SEX BY PRESCRIPTION

Dr. Thomas Szasz is a practicing psychiatrist, prolific author, and professor of psychiatry at the State University of New York at Syracuse. He lives in Manlius, New York.

Other books by Thomas Szasz

PAIN AND PLEASURE

THE MYTH OF MENTAL ILLNESS

LAW, LIBERTY, AND PSYCHIATRY

PSYCHIATRIC JUSTICE

THE ETHICS OF PSYCHOANALYSIS

THE MANUFACTURE OF MADNESS

IDEOLOGY AND INSANITY

THE AGE OF MADNESS (ED.)

THE SECOND SIN

CEREMONIAL CHEMISTRY

HERESIES

KARL KRAUS AND THE SOUL-DOCTORS

SCHIZOPHRENIA

PSYCHIATRIC SLAVERY

THE THEOLOGY OF MEDICINE

THE MYTH OF PSYCHOTHERAPY

Sex
by Prescription

THOMAS SZASZ

Penguin Books

Penguin Books Ltd, Harmondsworth,
Middlesex, England
Penguin Books, 625 Madison Avenue,
New York, New York 10022, U.S.A.
Penguin Books Australia Ltd, Ringwood,
Victoria, Australia
Penguin Books Canada Limited, 2801 John Street,
Markham, Ontario, Canada L3R 1B4
Penguin Books (N.Z.) Ltd, 182–190 Wairau Road,
Auckland 10, New Zealand

First published in the United States of America by
Anchor Press/Doubleday 1980
Published in Penguin Books by arrangement with
Doubleday & Company, Inc., 1981

Printed in the United States of America by
Offset Paperback Mfrs., Inc., Dallas, Pennsylvania
Set in Caledonia

FOR LYNN

Acknowledgments

I wish to thank everyone who has helped in the preparation of this book—especially my colleagues and friends, Sally Foster, Laura Neville, Ralph Raico, Anthony Trimarchi, and Lynn Wilcox; my brother, George Szasz, and my daughter, Susan Marie Szasz; my editors at Doubleday, Elizabeth Frost Knappman, Harriet Rubin, and Nora Titterington; the staff of the Library of the State University of New York, Upstate Medical Center, and my secretary, Barbara Svoboda.

Preface

Before the present century, when people spoke of "doctors" they were more likely to have in mind clerics than clinicians. Now it is the other way around. That metamorphosis, together with a reversal of values as blind as it is stubborn, epitomizes the basic change in the Western perspective on sex—from the days of the Church Fathers to those of the sex therapists.

"I was," wrote St. Augustine, "bound down by this disease of the flesh . . . that only you [God] can cure."[1] To the Great Doctor of Christianity in the fourth century, sexual desire was a disease; to the great doctors of coitus today, lack of sexual desire is a disease. "Inadequate sexual desire," asserts Helen Singer Kaplan, a professor of psychiatry at Cornell Medical Center and a prominent sex therapist, "is probably the most prevalent of the sexual dysfunctions."[2] Surely, among the achievements of modern education must be reckoned the fact that men and women who do not know the meaning of the word "concupiscence," *know*, nevertheless, that it is the unmistakable sign of freedom from the dread "diseases of desire" dear to the hearts of modern doctors of sexology.[3]

Doctors of theology and doctors of medicine, clerics

and clinicians, have much in common, especially when
it comes to sex. What they share, above all else, is an
arrogant certainty that they and they alone know how
God or Nature intends us to enjoy ourselves—sexually
and otherwise. Hence, they have always been, and apparently always will be, not great teachers, as their
name "doctor" implies, but great meddlers. From time
to time, clerics as well as clinicians have changed their
minds about what we must do to be in harmony with
the designs of God or Nature—but this has never
caused them to entertain the least doubt that they were
the proper interpreters and enforcers of those designs.
Sexual self-satisfaction (now usually called masturbation) is a good case in point.

Men and women—and, of course, children too—must
have always known that rubbing the genitals causes
pleasurable relief of sexual tension. Even some mam-
mals and primates have, through experience, discovered
this elementary piece of sex educational information.
"I wish to heaven," remarked the Greek philosopher
Diogenes (in the fourth century B.C.), "that I could
satisfy my hunger when my stomach barks for food by
rubbing it."[4] During the period ironically called the
Enlightenment, that piece of sexological insight was replaced by the medical dogma known as the "doctrine
of masturbatory insanity."[5] For more than two hundred
years—well into the twentieth century—the leaders of
Western science and thought maintained that masturbation caused a host of diseases and was itself a disease. Now they maintain that it cures a host of diseases
and that abstinence from it is a disease. Diogenes and
his contemporaries knew better: they understood that

desire, whether for food or sex, is not a disease; and
that the satisfaction of desire, whether it involves ali-
mentary or erotic acts, is not a treatment.

Eating and copulating have always been of interest
to people and are likely to remain so. Each of these behaviors satisfies a basic biological need—eating, the survival of the individual; copulating, the survival of the
species. Each may be a rich source of pleasure through
the gratification of desire—or a rich source of pain, for
many reasons, among them being diseases or conditions
believed to be diseases. Nutritional and sexual behaviors thus exhibit three faces: spiritual, sumptuary, and
hygienic. If we want to know what God permits or prohibits us from ingesting, we turn to rabbis and priests; if
we want to enhance our enjoyment of eating, we turn to
gourmet cooks; if we want relief from diseases of the
digestive system, we turn to doctors. Similarly, the
religious-ritual aspects of sex are the concern of the
clergyman and the theologian; the aesthetic-hedonic aspects of it are the concern of the poet and the pornog-
rapher;* the medical aspects of it—that is, the diseases
of the sexual organs and their treatment—are the concern of the physician.

Whether, when, with whom, and how a person
should engage in sexual acts depends on whether he
wants to please God, enhance his erotic enjoyment, or
promote his health. Hence, a question such as how

---

* Webster defines pornography as obscene or licentious writing or
painting. I use the term, here and elsewhere, nonpejoratively, to refer
to any sexually explicit writing. Cookbooks stimulate the appetite for
food. Sex books stimulate the appetite for sex. Sexologists from Krafft-
Ebing to Masters and Johnson have consistently denied this elementary fact, but have happily reaped the profits of pornography.

many orgasms a woman should have is like the question of how many children she should have. In the past, people in the Christian West believed that women should have as many children and as few orgasms as possible; now they believe just the opposite. These beliefs are important—but what, if anything, have they to do with medicine? To put it differently, what relationship, if any, is there between gourmet cooking and medicine, epicurean dining and diseases of the digestive system, pleasure in drinking and eating and psychiatry? The question is plainly absurd. Every educated person knows that if he wants to learn about good eating, he must consult Craig Claiborne, not his gastroenterologist; that doctors teach people how to abstain from eating and drinking, not how to enjoy these "indulgences."

When it comes to sex, however, such common sense vanishes. Everyone now *knows* that physicians, especially gynecologists and psychiatrists, are experts on sex. When people want to enjoy copulation or masturbation or some other erotic act, they turn to doctors to advise them. This folly rests on the belief that because physicians are knowledgeable about the physiology and pathology of the genital organs, they are experts on the experiencing and enjoying of the erotic passions as well.

Eating is a basic bodily function. We do not consider eating itself to be a disease or medical problem. We only consider certain disturbances in eating—such as occur, say, in cancer of the esophagus—to be the manifestations of a disease. And we do not assume that, because physicians are experts on esophageal cancer, they are also experts on questions such as whether people should eat with knives and forks or with chopsticks, sitting on chairs or reclining on sofas or carpets.

Like other bodily organs, the sexual organs are subject to disease. In addition, even in the absence of diseases affecting the genitals, the act of sexual intercourse gives rise to two conditions that people have often found undesirable and hence sought to prevent— namely, pregnancy and venereal disease. Since the prevention of conception and infectious disease requires medical knowledge, the physician must, indeed, be intimately involved in matters sexual. This is why contraception and the prevention and treatment of venereal diseases have formed two of the portals through which the physician entered the area of human sexuality. A third portal—perhaps the most important one for modern sexology—was formed by so-called disturbances of the sexual function, such as impotence and frigidity.

What, exactly, are impotence and frigidity? How shall we view them, understand them, "treat" them? Impotence—the inability to have or sustain an erection —can be the manifestation of a disease, say of multiple sclerosis; or it can be the manifestation of a man's conscience, say of his belief that certain (or all) sexual acts are wrong and forbidden. Frigidity—the woman's inability to enjoy certain (or all) sexual acts—can likewise be a manifestation of either a medical or a moral condition. In other words, the presence or absence of appetite, whether for food or sexual satisfaction, depends both on the condition of the *body* and the character of the *person*. We are expected to develop an aversion to eating the flesh of cats or dogs or human beings and hence would not consider a lack of salivary or gastric arousal for such foods, even if we were hungry, the manifestation of a disorder of the digestive system. Lack of sexual arousal in certain situations is usually a similar affair, signifying the person's true feelings about the matter. The penis, some wag has observed, never lies. But sexologists do—principally because they are determined to conceal moral values and social policies as medical diagnoses and treatments. "Scientific" sexology is a veritable Trojan horse: appearing to be modernity's gift to mankind in its struggle for freedom and dignity, it is, in fact, just another strategy for its pacification and enslavement.

Contents

Sexual Medicine

1

SEX AND THE SELF

Sex is a body-contact sport. It is safe to watch but more
fun to play. Although sex is a risky game, one is supposed to pretend that it is not. Yet it is the dangerousness, rather than the mysteriousness, of the game
that provides sex "experts" their many followers. Promising to teach people how to play the sex game well,
sexologists seduce them into believing that they can
teach them how to play it safely—which, of course, no
one can do. Why? Because the dangerousness of
human sexuality lies in the fact that sexual acts are so
very personal. Behaving sexually toward another person is risky because doing so is profoundly self-
revealing and because the needs of the participants are
constantly changing and are rarely fully complemen-
tary.* There is simply no way to avoid this. It is the

* This is why sexual bonding can be such a powerful force for fos-
tering social cooperation, and why solitary (masturbatory) sex is so
popular with modern sex educators.

way life is—a somber reminder, perhaps, that the
human sexual constitution did not evolve to its present
form to make intercourse between the sexes harmo-
nious.

Next to the need for sleep, water, and food, the sexual urge is our most powerful biological drive. Nevertheless, neither releasing this drive nor inhibiting it
constitutes or causes disease.† This remarkable fact
alone ought to make us skeptical about contemporary
medical claims concerning the pathology and therapy
of sexual dysfunctions. Yet, the very acceptance of such
terms as "sexual dysfunction," "sexual disorder," and
"sexual pathology" makes us believe that such conditions exist.

Our language informs and even defines our percep-
tions. When we talk about sexual dysfunctions the im-
plication is that the labels for such alleged disorders
name abnormal sexual conditions that exist—in the
same sense in which, say, cancer of the colon exists.
This is simply not true.

Illustrative of the blinders that our language places
on our view of human sexuality is the fact that we have
only a single term for the pleasurable experience associated with the relief of sexual tension. Because of
this verbal constraint, sexologists write as if there were
an orgasm or orgastic experience that is always the
same—even for men and women. But this is contrary to
common sense and common experience. A person does
not have the same pleasure every time he eats the same

† I am disregarding here the risk of acquiring venereal disease,
which stands in the same relation to sex as the risk of acquiring food-
borne infection stands to eating.

food or drinks the same drink—regardless of how much he likes these substances. Moreover, although our body is primed to feel sexual pleasure, we must nevertheless acquire the experience through learning. Just as we do not all react to music or food in the same way, we do not react to sex in the same way. The varieties of human sexual experience are, indeed, as rich and varied as the varieties of human religious experience.‡[1]

Some parallels between eating and sex may help us see contemporary sexological claims in a clearer light. Let us look upon eating as if it were an oro-gastric performance—that is, a set of actions performed by our mouth, salivary and gastric glands, esophagus, and stomach. What are the various oro-gastric performances that might be displayed by a hungry person confronted with the possibility of eating a certain food—say, oysters? We need to know neither gastroenterology (that is, about diseases of the digestive tract) nor gastronomy (that is, about the art of good eating) to recognize that such a person's reaction is likely to fall into one or another of the following four categories: he may refuse to eat oysters and be perfectly happy about it; he may seemingly accept the oysters, but, unable to "stomach" them, he may gag on them; he may accept the oysters and get them down, but

‡ *The Homosexual Matrix* by C. A. Tripp offers a rich display of the fundamental similarities between religion and sex—between how human beings worship gods and each other. For example, the following observation made by Tripp (not intended by him to make this point) applies to religious practices even more than to sexual practices: "A fair judgment of what other people do [sexually] requires the utmost caution—all the more so since each and every sex technique is destined to seem ridiculous to those for whom it has no value."[2]

without any pleasure; or he may eagerly desire oysters, savor them slowly, and delight in eating them. None of these is considered to be a medical matter: we have no Greco-Latin diagnostic names to attach to such attitudes toward food.

Let us look upon heterosexual intercourse in the male similarly—as if it were a performance by the penis. What are the various sexual performances that might be displayed by a sexually hungry man confronted with the possibility of engaging in a certain sexual act—say, intercourse with a beautiful, sexually experienced, and willing woman? Again, we need not be experts on sex to recognize that such a man's reactions are likely to fall into one or another of some familiar categories: he may reject the sexual opportunity as morally unacceptable and be perfectly happy about it; he may try to engage in intercourse but find himself unable to achieve an erection; he may have an erection, but ejaculate promptly after penetration or even prior to it; he may have an erection, penetrate, but feel as if his penis were anesthetized and be unable to ejaculate; finally, he may engage in a highly stimulating and satisfying act of sexual intercourse. While all this is rather obvious, by cataloguing these sexual patterns we see that whereas our language attaches no labels of illness-and-health to the various reactions a man has toward an object of food, it does attach such labels to the various reactions he has toward a "sex object."* Thus, for more than a century, terms such as "impotence,"

---

* Because the language of medicine or sexology medicalizes and dehumanizes, it is quite useless for giving an account of the sexual lives of men and women as persons. It is useful, however, for presenting human beings as sexual cripples, idiots, or degenerates.

"premature ejaculation," and "retarded ejaculation"
have been accepted as the names of certain abnormal
or pathological conditions affecting the so-called male
sexual apparatus or male sexual functions. This is sheer
nonsense. I am not saying, of course, that the sexual
performances I have described do not actually occur or
are not real. I deny only that these phenomena are *ipso
facto* medical diseases or problems.[3]

However, *some* of these phenomena *may* be due to
organic diseases or the effects of drugs. Impotence, in
particular, may be due to congenital malformation of
the penis (which is rare); to injury to the nerves sup-
plying the genitals (which may be a complication, or
unavoidable side effect, of pelvic or urogenital surgery); to certain systemic diseases (for example, diabetes, severe arteriosclerosis, leukemia); and to certain
drugs (for example, alcohol, anti-hypertensives, psy-
cho-active agents). Frigidity may have similar causes.
The traditional distinction between organic and psychogenic sexual disorders remains of paramount importance.† Throughout the book, unless otherwise noted,
I am addressing myself only to the latter group of phenomena—that is, to so-called sexual dysfunctions displayed by persons with healthy bodies, or with diseases
that do not impair their sexual abilities.

Failure of the heart, the lung, or the liver to perform
its function is always considered a disease, in men as

---

† A new diagnostic procedure—the measurement of "nocturnal penile
tumescence" (erection during sleep)—promises to offer an objective
method for differentiating between organic and psychogenic impotence.[4]

well as women. This is not always true for failure of the
sexual organs to perform theirs: some such nonfunc-
tions do not count as a disease at all, while others may
count as a disease for one sex but not the other. A
quick review of currently accepted sexual (coital) disorders will illustrate this point.

1. The person wants to perform sexually—or believes and declares that he or she wants to—but is
unable to do so: in men this is called impotence; in
women, vaginismus. The term "frigidity" should
not be applied to this condition, though sometimes
it is, because women can engage in an essentially
passive kind of sexual performance (that is, without genital activity). This is why in the woman,
unconscious rejection of the sexual act is manifested by a *stiffening* of the vaginal muscles—
whereas in the man, who must be genitally active
to perform sexually, it is manifested by a *softening*
of the penile shaft.

2. The person's sexual performance is deemed
to be too quick: in men this is called premature
ejaculation (ejaculatio praecox); in women it is
not considered to be an illness and is not named.

3. The person's sexual performance is deemed to
be too slow: in men this is called retarded ejaculation (ejaculatio retardata); in women this is usually not considered to be an illness and is not
named—or it may be called frigidity.

4. The sexual performance is normal, but the
performer experiences no pleasure: in women this

is called frigidity or anorgasmia; in men this was, until recently, not considered to be an illness, but is now also called anorgasmia.

5. Sexual acts are deliberately avoided and the subject regards his or her nonperformance as meritorious; this is called chastity in both men and women (and it may or may not be considered an illness).

Instead of regarding sexual dysfunctions as diseases, we could more profitably regard them as the solutions of certain life tasks—that is, as the expressions of the individual's life-style. Consider, for example, the man who completes the sex act very quickly (which Kinsey regarded as normal, but which is now conventionally called premature ejaculation). The man himself may be dissatisfied with his performance, or he may not be. We might look upon him as we do on a man whose idea of eating a meal is to gulp down a hamburger and french fries in three minutes flat. Such a person is assuredly no gourmet: he does not know how to eat like a gourmet— that is, how to stretch a seven-course meal with drinks over three hours and enjoy every minute of it. Similarly, the quick sexual performer is not a sexual gourmet: he does not know—for whatever reason—how to have leisurely sex. If he wants to change this, he must learn new patterns of sexual performance. This task can be achieved in many ways—ranging from self-help through reading, practice, and the assistance of experienced and sympathetic sexual partners to a variety of systems of counseling, psychotherapy, or so-called sex therapy. Although I am generally critical of, and skep-

tical toward, professional approaches to sexual problems, nothing that I say in this book is intended to
imply that all medical, psychological, or psychiatric
help for persons who seek such assistance for their sexual difficulties is worthless.

We must remember that, in its day, exorcism
"worked" too. That it worked is a fact—but that fact
does not prove that the persons so helped were possessed by demons. Certain new (as well as old) sex
therapies work—in the sense that they may enable some
persons to engage in sexual activities more freely, com-
petently, or pleasurably than they could previously. It
does not follow, however, that this proves the validity
of the sex therapists' claims about their ideas or interventions. The mode of action of the new sex therapies
is easily explained along simple, common-sense lines.
Clients seeking sex therapy accept their therapists as
authorities—as expert healers, physicians, scientists.
This enables the experts to grant patients absolution
for sexual ignorance or ineptness, and permission to engage in sexual acts that they formerly feared or considered forbidden. Saying more than this about why all
manner of human interventions might, or might not,
help persons now identified as suffering from sexual
dysfunctions invites a digression I want to resist here.[5]

Because human beings are boundlessly imaginative
and inventive, they can perform sexual acts of a surprising variety. Thus, there are many ways of giving
and gaining sexual stimulation and satisfaction, and
many of them are now widely advertised in sex man-
uals. Besides the genitals, the main anatomical parts

and physiological functions used for sexual purposes in our culture are the eyes and ears; vision, speech, and hearing; the hands and fingers; the breasts and nipples; the mouth and tongue; the anus; the skin, anywhere on the body. In addition, there is a vast array of artifacts used as sexual aids or instruments, ranging from pornography to vibrators.

Despite the increasing cultural dissociation between procreative and recreative sexuality, the male and female genitals remain the organs most widely used in performing sexual acts. With respect to these organs, men and women differ—notwithstanding the attempts of modern sex researchers to obscure or deny these differences. So far as heterosexual coitus is concerned, its performance requires an erect penis capable of insertion into the vagina on the part of the male, and a penetrable vagina on the part of the female. These physical facts play a major role in determining the duration of coitus. If the penis remained erect after the man's orgasm, as the vagina remains penetrable after the woman's, then the timing of the ejaculation would not have the significance it has. Indeed, the concept of premature ejaculation has no correlate in the female, in whom a swift orgastic response in heterosexual coitus is today regarded very positively indeed. So, while a quick orgastic response in the male is now regarded as a manifestation of sexual incompetence, the same response in the female is regarded as a manifestation of sexual competence.

While premature ejaculation has no correlate in the female, retarded ejaculation (retarded orgasm) is analogous to frigidity. Again, this sort of performance may or may not be undesirable for one or both partners. As premature ejaculation acquires its significance from the fact that heterosexual coitus cannot continue after the man ejaculates, so retarded ejaculation acquires its significance from the fact that the act cannot cease (is not expected to cease) until the man ejaculates. Premature ejaculation embarrasses the man. Delayed ejaculation embarrasses the woman (unless intravaginal ejaculation cannot occur at all, which is likely to embarrass both partners). If the partners were free to end coitus without ejaculation, then retarded ejaculation might be welcomed by the woman and be no problem for the man. Furthermore, these problems would not occur if the heterosexual act were not limited to the use of the genitals as the principal organs for giving and receiving sexual stimulation. The imagery and idiom of impotence and vaginismus do not apply to nongenital sexual acts, as the following simple examples illustrate.

A man who cannot have an erection—in what is conventionally considered to be a sexually stimulating situation—is said to be impotent. But a man who cannot bring himself to make oral or manual contact with a woman's genitals is not regarded as having a namable sexual dysfunction. Similarly, while the woman who rejects male penetration by constriction of the vaginal muscles is said to be exhibiting vaginismus, the woman who rejects fellatio and gags at the very thought of it is not considered to be manifesting any kind of sexual disorder.

Here is another example. Children and most women can resort to crying as a means of easing the pain of disappointment, grief, or unhappiness. Most men can-

not do so—because, in a profound sense, they do not
want to do so: they have learned that crying is "un-
manly." Similarly, many women have learned that
being sexually self-affirmative is "unfeminine": hence,
they are unable to discharge sexual tension through
(coital) orgasm. Such women are now called anorgas-
mic (they used to be called frigid), but men who cannot weep are not called alachrymal. The former condition is considered to be a sexual dysfunction, but the
latter is not considered to be a lachrymal dysfunction.

Although the definitions of abnormal bodily functions and abnormal behaviors both come down to culturally conditioned human judgments, there is an important difference between these two classes of
phenomena. Dysfunctions of the heart, liver, and kid-
ney are disorders of the human *body*. They can be
diagnosed objectively, and can be treated by interventions imposed by a physician upon the patient's
body. The same is true for disorders of the genital organs—for example, gonorrhea. But this is not true for
so-called sexual dysfunctions, which are "disorders" of
the human *self*. Such disorders cannot be diagnosed
objectively—the subject's (or his or her partner's) testimony being necessary for the diagnosis. Nor can they
be treated by interventions imposed by a physician
upon the patient's body, the "therapy" requiring the
active participation of the subject in the remedial procedure. Sex therapy resembles learning much more
closely than it does the ordinary chemical or surgical
treatment of disease.[6] Finally, the results of treating
sexual disorders, like their diagnosis, are subjective,
resting largely on the subject's self-assessment. For

these reasons, and for others to be discussed in subsequent chapters, much of the professional literature about the diagnosis and treatment of sexual dysfunctions is misleading—or worse.

2

SEX AS DISEASE

Being in close touch with divinities, divines were long recognized as experts on sin and were accorded special privileges and powers to punish the sinners. For millennia, priests were thus the accepted authorities on what counted as sinful sexual behavior—with consequences all too familiar to any educated person.

Now it is the clinicians who, being in close touch with medical science, are recognized as experts on sickness and are accorded special privileges and powers to diagnose and treat the sick. Since the birth of modern medicine, in the seventeenth century, the physician has become the accepted authority on what counts as sick sexual behavior—with consequences surprisingly unfamiliar to most people.

Christian theologians quickly developed a powerful penchant for declaring that all sex is sinful. Once recognized as medical authorities, the doctors did not lag far behind: they "discovered" that sex was, for the most part, a disease or an important cause of disease. (In recent decades, the doctors turned their discovery around by one hundred and eighty degrees: now they claim that sex is a treatment.)

In the seventeenth century, female sexuality, formerly viewed as immoral, became viewed as unhealthy. Some French physicians maintained that any sexual excitement in women is "a melancholic affliction," while others stigmatized the "open display of sexual desire" as a sure sign of mental disease.[1] A typical case from that period concerns a young French woman who developed a "sexual excitement" after she had had a clandestine love affair with someone below her station, to whom her parents refused to give the nod. "When a doctor was called, he had the girl confined in a French Medical Torture house [carnificina] where after bloodletting, repeated 30 times in six days, he drew from the girl along with her blood at the same time her insane mind, mad love, dear life."[2] Drawing from the victim "dear life"—that is, medical murder—was evidently considered to be an appropriate treatment for nymphomania.

Next, the doctors turned their attention to masturbation. The idea that masturbation poses grave medical hazards was an eighteenth-century discovery. For the next two hundred years, the concept of masturbatory insanity—that is, the view that masturbation causes or is a symptom of madness—dominated medical science as well as the popular imagination.[3] People believed that masturbation was harmful for many of the same reasons that they believed that blood-letting was helpful: sperm was seen as precious and hence in need of preservation, whereas the blood of the sick was seen as poisonous and hence in need of elimination. The long history of anti-masturbation reflects this fundamental fallacy.

Benjamin Rush (1746–1813), a leading physician of his time and the father of American psychiatry, was a fanatic advocate of bleeding as a panacea and of anti-masturbation as a prophylactic. "Masturbation," he asserted in 1812, "produces seminal weakness, impotence, dysury, tabes dorsalis, pulmonary consumption, dyspepsia, dimness of sight, vertigo, epilepsy, hypochondriasis, loss of memory, managlia, fatuity, and death."[4]

In French psychiatry, which played so crucial a role in the history of this discipline, it was Jean-Étienne Esquirol (1772–1840) who embraced the masturbatory hypothesis and placed upon it the stamp of his authority. Esquirol claimed no originality for having discovered the pathogenic effects of masturbation; quite the contrary. In 1816, he declared that "Masturbation is recognized in all countries as a common cause of insanity."[5] In 1822, he added: "[Masturbation] is a grave symptom in mania; unless it stops at once, it is an insurmountable obstacle to cure. By lowering the powers of resistance it reduces the patient to a state of stupidity . . . and death."* [6] Backed by the authority of men

* These views were repeated and extended in Esquirol's classic textbook, *Des maladies mentales*, published in 1838. "Masturbation [he wrote] may be a forerunner of mania, of dementia, and even of senile dementia; it leads to melancholy and suicide; its consequences are more serious in men than in women; it is a grave obstacle to cure in those of the insane who frequently resort to it during their illness."[7]

like Rush and Esquirol, the so-called masturbatory hypothesis quickly spread across the face of the civilized world.

Mid-nineteenth-century American medical opinion on masturbation is best illustrated by this editorial comment in the *New Orleans Medical and Surgical Journal:* "[N]either plague, nor war, nor smallpox, nor a crowd of similar evils, have resulted more disastrously for humanity than the habit of masturbation: it is the destroying element of civilized society."[8]

One of the most popular late-nineteenth-century American books of medical advice was *The People's Common Sense Medical Adviser* by R. V. Pierce. By 1895, it was in its seventy-first edition and had sold more than 2,300,000 copies. Pierce lists "Spermatorrhea (Seminal Weakness)" as a disease that is "induced by the early habit of masturbation," and that "enfeebles the constitution, and results in impotency, premature decline . . . [etc.], softening of the brain, and insanity."[9] Pierce warns the reader against quacks who claim to be able to cure spermatorrhea, and cautions that although "The general practitioner may be thoroughly read in these diseases, he cannot acquire the skill of a specialist who annually treats thousands of cases. . . ."[10] The chapter ends on twelve pages of testimonials from the grateful patients cured of spermatorrhea.

The doctrine of masturbatory insanity laid the foundations for the progressive medicalization of sex that began in earnest toward the end of the last century. The two men whose works have contributed most significantly to this development were Richard von Krafft-Ebing and Sigmund Freud.

Krafft-Ebing (1840–1902) was a psychiatrist best remembered for his magnum opus, *Psychopathia Sexualis*. First published in 1886, the book was an enormous success. Despite the author's deliberate use of Latin words to de-erotize lurid passages, it sold widely to the public. Interestingly, an unexpurgated edition of *Psychopathia Sexualis*, with all words translated into English, did not appear until 1965.

Psychopathia Sexualis is full of falsehoods pretentiously presented as if they were the fruits of hard-won scientific discoveries. Krafft-Ebing's claim that "Anomalies of the sexual functions are met with especially in civilized races"[11]—a claim contradicted by the Old Testament itself—is a typical example of such pseudoscientific fraud. Without any evidence for it, Krafft-Ebing also maintained that "sexual anomalies" are, in large part, inherited diseases of the central nervous system.[12]

Krafft-Ebing's case histories, though at once boring and lurid, also support the view that his aim was to separate sick (dirty) sexual perverts from healthy (clean) persons whose sexual practices were restrained and purely procreative. The titles of his case histories are illustrative: Exhibitionist; Defilers of Statues; Rape and Lust Murder; Unnatural Abuse; Violation of Animals; Zooerasty; Letter from an Urning; A Woman-Hater's Ball in Berlin; Various Categories of Male-Loving Men; Necrophilia. His attitude toward these sexual acts—indeed, toward sexuality in general—may be inferred from his views on masturbation. That practice,

he asserted, "despoils the unfolding bud of perfume
and beauty, and leaves behind only the coarse, animal
desire for sexual satisfaction. . . . The glow of sensual
sensibility wanes, and the inclination toward the opposite sex is weakened."[13]

In short, Krafft-Ebing, the founder of modern sexology, moved not one inch beyond the entrenched position of the earlier nineteenth-century doctors and their
doctrine of masturbatory insanity. He was not interested in liberating men and women from the shackles
of sexual prejudice or the constraints of anti-sexual leg-
islation. On the contrary, he was interested in supplant-
ing the waning power of the church with the waxing
power of medicine. "The physician," wrote Krafft-Ebing, "finds, perhaps, a solace in the fact that he may at
times refer those manifestations which offend against
our ethical or aesthetical principles to a diseased condition of the mind or the body."[14] Yet, because he wrote
about sex when polite society was silent about it, and
because he wrote about it as if it were a disease or
medical problem, Krafft-Ebing has been mistaken as a
progressive force in the struggle against sexual prejudice and prudery.

Sigmund Freud (1856–1939), the founder of psychoanalysis, is likewise regarded as a sexual revolutionary.
But Freud did not believe in individual sexual self-determination. His sexual prejudices—which he glorified
by calling them a "psychoanalytic theory of sex"†—

† Besides offering some elementary descriptions and fanciful specu-
lations about sexual development in children, Freud's "theory of sexuality" comes down to a very simple idea—namely, that human sexuality

reveal that he viewed sex either as a disease or as a treatment. His opinions on masturbation are illustrative. For example, in 1898 Freud restates the traditional anti-masturbatory doctrine, asserting: "If masturbation is the cause of neurasthenia [a popular psychiatric diagnosis at that time], then the prevention of masturbation in both sexes is a task that deserves more attention than it has hitherto received."[15]

The enormous importance that Freud and the early Freudians attributed to masturbation is illustrated by the fact that, between 1908 and 1912, thirteen meetings of the Vienna Psychoanalytic Society were devoted to discussions of this subject. The proceedings of these meetings reveal that the view that masturbation causes neurosis had, by this time, hardened into psychoanalytic dogma.[16] At the end of the deliberations, in 1912, Freud concludes that masturbation is an "infantile sexual activity" which is definitely a cause of "neurosis" and possibly of "organic injury" as well.[17]

Furthermore, Freud saw masturbation not only in sexual self-stimulation but also in all sorts of nongenital, nonsexual activities. For example, in his paper on "The Unconscious" (1915), Freud mentions the case of a young man whose skin was blemished by blackheads which he liked to evacuate, a common enough practice

---

is a losing proposition. As Freud saw it, men and women can engage in "normal" (genital-procreative) sexual acts—as a result of which they are likely to get babies, which most people most of the time do not want. Or they can engage in "abnormal" (perverse) sexual acts—as a result of which women get hysteria and men get neurasthenia. Or men can engage in sexual acts with prostitutes—as a result of which they are likely to get syphilis. In short, sex is more trouble than it is worth.

among adolescents. Freud's interpretation of this behavior is that "Pressing out the contents of the blackheads is clearly to him a substitute for masturbation.
The cavity which then appears owing to his fault is the
female genital, i.e., the fulfillment of the threat of castration (or the phantasy representing the threat) pro-
voked by his masturbation."[18] Among the countless
other acts that meant masturbation to Freud were rituals, compulsions, and obsessions.[19]

Like their prophet, Freud, psychoanalysts think of
themselves as experts on sex and as individuals espous-
ing daringly progressive positions on sex. Such a claim
has no basis in fact. On the contrary, psychoanalysts
have continued to regard unconventional sexual behavior as illness—which they are especially adept at
diagnosing and treating.

According to Karl Menninger, one of the most
influential post-Freudian psychoanalysts in America,
"masturbation occasions a heavy burden of guilt, because in the unconscious mind it always represents ag-
gression against someone."[20] Menninger does not claim
that masturbation is physically harmful. He claims, instead, that it is psychologically harmful because it
always represents an unjustified attack on another
person, and therefore provokes guilt in the actor.
Menninger does not explain why masturbation is an attack on other people, while eating, drinking, urinating,
and defecating are not.

Psychoanalysts are now defending the disease concept of various "perverse" sexual practices as if they
were valuable possessions of which they are being

robbed. In a way, that, of course, is exactly the case. While masturbation qua disease is defended by Menninger (and others, as we shall see), homosexuality qua disease is defended by Socarides (and others). A professor of clinical psychiatry at the State University of New York in Brooklyn, and a prominent psychoanalyst, Charles Socarides cites the conclusions of a task force of psychiatrists as evidence of the "fact that exclusive homosexuality [is] a disorder of psychosexual development."[21] While this view is not exactly novel, Socarides' interpretation of the objection of homosexuals against being called mentally sick is. He writes: "In response to legal and social persecution, homosexual groups began in the sixties not only to turn on their persecutors, but also to turn against their medical (psychiatric) protectors who offered help and hope."[22] It is difficult to know whether to call such a statement bizarre, ludicrous, or a bad joke. But Socarides is serious. Lamenting the American Psychiatric Association's 1973 decision to delete homosexuality from its official list of mental diseases, he remarks: "The consequences of this action are of a formidable nature. Not only will the homosexual be victimized, but the entire area of research in the development of gender-identity will be damaged."[23] Such pronouncements illustrate the psychiatrist's stubborn and selfish belief that certain sexual behaviors can be investigated scientifically, and treated humanely, only if they are called diseases.

However, regardless of how compassionate or liberated psychoanalysts pretend to be, they are dead set against recognizing the rights of persons, especially of women, to their genitals. In 1973, there appeared a paper in *The Journal of the American Psychoanalytic Association* entitled "On a Particular Form of Masturbation in Women: Masturbation with Water." Although this type of masturbation is taken for granted in the pages of *Cosmopolitan, Playboy,* and *Penthouse,* Eugene Halpert, the author of this scientific paper, thought it was so unusual that it deserved a special study. He called the phenomenon "a specific, unusual form of masturbation in the female," and sought to answer the "basic question of why these particular women chose this solution to their unconscious conflicts. . . ."[24] Halpert's choice of words in phrasing his question predetermines his answer. Looking for unconscious conflicts for which masturbation is a solution, rather than for personal reasons for choosing a particular method for relieving sexual tension, Halpert found what he was looking for—Freudian castration trauma and penis envy: "Women who masturbate by running water over their clitoris are using this form of masturbation to express the supplementary fantasies: I have my father's penis and can urinate/ejaculate like a man, and I am able to urinate and destroy/castrate with my powerful stream in revenge for castration."[25] If female masturbation with water expresses the fantasy that the woman wants to be a man, what fantasy does male masturbation express when the masturbator uses certain objects as substitutes for the vagina—as described, for example, in *Portnoy's Complaint?*[26] No doubt the interpretation that such masturbation expresses the fantasy of having a vagina—in fact, one's mother's vagina—and hence constitutes a manifestation of "vagina

envy," awaits only confirmation by the results of further psychoanalytic research into the psychopathology
of male masturbation.

These examples illustrate the stubborn determination of many psychiatrists to resist the idea that people have a right to masturbate. Emblematic of the psychoanalysts' continuing denial of that right, especially
to women, is the review of *The Hite Report* in the *Journal of the American Psychoanalytic Association*. The
author of the *Report*, Shere Hite, claims that the organ
of female sexual responsiveness is not the receptacle
that fits the penis in intercourse, but the clitoris.[27] She
links this finding, in itself not exactly a novelty, to a
firm and well-reasoned rejection of the masculine right
to define the norms of feminine sexuality. It was precisely Hite's insistence that women have the same right
to sexual self-definition as do men that most enraged
the psychoanalysts. "It is a slanted book, openly angry,
didactic, and exhortatory," complains the reviewer.
"Ms. Hite's central and often repeated thesis is that
women should free themselves from male definitions of
female sexuality and male prescriptions of how sex
should be done."[28] But what is wrong with that thesis?
The reviewer never tells us, leaving us with the impression that he thinks only Freud has the right to tell
women "how sex should be done."

Psychiatrists and psychoanalysts can accept the idea
that the clitoris might receive stimulation indirectly
during intercourse but frown at the idea of deliberate
clitoral stimulation. They thus miss the point of books
such as *The Hite Report*—the rejection of the (male)

professional as sexual expert. By rightly emphasizing the moral and political aspects of sexual acts, Hite and other feminists are seeking to topple the physician from his position as sexual legislator.

3

SEX AS TREATMENT— IN THEORY

Until the middle of this century, sexologists painted sex in the dark colors of disease. This established sex as a legitimate medical concern and set the stage for the present scene in which sex is painted in the glowing colors of treatment. Although many people have contributed to this phase of sexology,* William Masters' work is emblematic of it.

* A seventeenth-century French physician wrote confidently that the cure of hysterical symptoms is "easy when the remedy of Venus is applied."[1] One of the earliest German psychiatric texts, published in 1803, mentions sexual intercourse quite matter of factly, as if it were a well-established method of psychiatric treatment: "The most powerful and most pleasant bodily sensations derive from sleeping with a person of the opposite sex. Chiarugi maintains that it is an excellent cure for melancholia."[2]

Masters began his sexological studies in 1954, working with professional prostitutes as his subjects. In 1957, he replaced himself with the "team" of Masters and Johnson, and replaced the prostitutes with volunteers. Over a period of twelve years, these subjects produced for Masters, and displayed before him, "more than 10,000 orgasms."[3]

Who are Masters and Johnson? William Howell Masters was born in Cleveland in 1915. He graduated from the University of Rochester School of Medicine, went on to specialize in obstetrics and gynecology, and was for some years on the faculty of the Washington University School of Medicine in St. Louis, Missouri. In 1954, Masters founded the Reproductive Biology Research Foundation, which became, in 1978, the Masters and Johnson Foundation.

Virginia Eshelman Johnson was born in Missouri in 1925 and graduated from high school in 1941. In 1951 she married George Johnson, had two children, and divorced him in 1956. Before joining Masters in his sex research in 1957, her main interest and talent seemed to have been singing. Johnson has earned no degree higher than a high school diploma, but calls herself a psychologist.

Masters and Johnson rose to instant fame in 1966 with the publication of their first book, *Human Sexual Response.*[4] *Time* magazine ran a feature story about the authors, with a photograph showing Dr. Masters and Mrs. Johnson in white laboratory coats, microscope in the foreground, gazing at a chart. The story told about their investigations at the Reproductive Biology Research Foundation in St. Louis, concluding that

these were "helping to make it possible for supposedly
infertile couples to have children, helping to prolong
the enjoyment of a healthy and normal sex life for
aging couples at least into their 80's."[5] Such praise was
typical of the mass media response accorded to Masters
and Johnson.

Perhaps because Masters deals with sex, a subject
about which people are insecure and hence gullible; or
perhaps because he presents himself so adroitly as a
medical investigator, a pioneer as well as an authority,
Masters has been extremely successful in convincing
both professionals and the public of the importance
and validity of his claims. To be sure, there have been
some criticisms of certain of his observations and rec-
ommendations. But there has been no criticism of his
entire work on the ground that it is not a medical or
therapeutic but a moral and political enterprise. For
example, Edward M. Brecher, a respected science
writer, lavishes praise on Masters for his studies in the
physiology of the sexual response and the therapy of
sexual inadequacy and attributes Masters' achievements to his adopting toward human sexuality "the
kind of attitude that scientists customarily hold toward digestion, circulation, and other physiological phenomena."[6]

But scientists who study the physiology of digestion
do not train men and women with unsophisticated
tastes and eating habits to be gourmets and would not
call doing so digestion therapy. The fact that Masters'
observations—revealing that sexual arousal causes the
penis to become erect and the vagina to lubricate, and
that such arousal can, under certain circumstances,

lead to the pleasurable relief of sexual tension—have at-
tracted so much attention testifies to the perennial interest in pornography (especially if it is made legitimate by being couched in medical terms). Actually,
these clinical investigations are merely a screen for
concealing Masters' moral judgments and political pro-
posals. Masters has, simply, consolidated the medical
conquest of human sexuality. How he has done so may
be best appreciated, to begin with, by examining his
(and Johnson's) writing style.

One of the most obvious characteristics of Masters
and Johnson's prose style is the absence of terms identifying persons as individuals, whether they be therapists
or patients. They refer to themselves as "the team" or
"the Foundation," and to their patients as "the couple," "the relationship," or "the unit," as in the following sentence: "It should be emphasized that the foundation's basic premise of therapy insists that, although
both husband and wife in a sexually dysfunctional marriage are to be treated, the marital relationship is considered as the patient."[7]

This piece of pseudo-English gives us a glimpse of
the real ugliness—at once linguistic and spiritual—of
Masters and Johnson's work. Here is a sentence that
carefully eliminates persons from both sides of the
therapeutic relationship. Indeed, the therapist is not
even the Foundation—but the "basic premise." "The
basic premise," we are told, "insists." On what? On
claiming that neither husband nor wife is the patient,
but that the marital relationship is. That simply cannot
be so. When people consult Masters and Johnson, they

usually pay for the service they receive. When a check is made out for the payment, it is written and signed by a person (or persons), not by a "marital relationship."†

Another of their favorite words is "professional," as in their first sentence in the Acknowledgments in *Human Sexual Inadequacy:* "We are deeply indebted to the professionals who have worked with us. . . ."[10] Does that include the professional prostitutes? Does it include the woman physician to whose contributions they offer this fulsome praise:

> . . . a physician, frankly quite curious about the partner-surrogate role, offered her services to evaluate the potentials (if any) of the role. When convinced of the desperate need for such a partner in the treatment of sexual dysfunction in the unmarried male, she continued as a partner surrogate, contributing both personal and professional experiences to develop the role to a peak of effectiveness. The therapists are indeed more than indebted to this intelligent woman. [Why not "doctor," doctor?] Many of her suggestions as to personal approaches and psychosocially supportive techniques are original contributions to the therapeutic process.[11]

Surely this must be one of the greatest put-ons in modern scientific writing. Projecting the image of the

† Masters and Johnson's obsession with the "couple" as the "unit"[8] is in the grand tradition of early nineteenth-century French socialist-utopian thinkers, exemplified by Charles Fourier (1772–1837). A failed businessman turned social planner, Fourier dreamed of organizing the whole world into mutually cooperating "phalanxes," each such group consisting of four hundred families of four persons each. Central to the theory of Fourierism was the denial of the reality of actual individuals, and the defining of "the couple"—that is, man and woman—as "the true social individual."[9]

doctor as self-sacrificing hero—in the best tradition of
the bacteriologist inoculating himself with yellow
fever!—Masters and Johnson here reveal that one of
their "surrogate partners" was a female physician. She
did it all for the love of science, of course.

The distinctive peculiarities of Masters and Johnson's prose style have been remarked on by others, notably by Paul Robinson, who has called *Human Sexual
Response* and *Human Sexual Inadequacy* "undoubt-
edly two of the worst written books in the English
language."[12] After listing and giving examples of some
of Masters and Johnson's major linguistic "offenses
against both sense and elegance," Robinson concluded
that much of what they say is "nonsense."[13] It is that,
but it is also something else. As George Orwell noted,
the bureaucratic style—which is Masters and Johnson's
ideal—reeks not only of pomposity, but also of insincerity.[14] Actually, Masters and Johnson's prose style is
carefully cultivated—ostensibly to "avoid any possible
suggestion of pornography": *"Human Sexual Response,"* Masters told an interviewer in 1969, "is hard
reading on purpose. . . . We even rewrote the book to
make it as obtuse as possible."[15] In their own distinctive way, then, Masters and Johnson are great stylists:
They are the foremost base rhetoricians of modern sexology.[16] I mean by that that they are skillful in concealing and communicating their sexual ethic and sexual
prescriptions as if these were the results of their "scientific research" and the products of their "professional"
expertise. The upshot is that many of their positions on

practical sexual questions as well as their general sexual ethics are internally inconsistent.‡

For example, Masters and Johnson like to pretend that they are the supreme sexual egalitarians: They emphasize the basic similarities not only between male and female sexuality but also between heterosexual and homosexual acts. This posture, however, is inconsistent with their justification of the dual-sex team method—namely, that men cannot understand the sexuality of women, and vice versa. Claiming that "controlled laboratory experimentation in human sexual physiology has supported unequivocally the initial investigative premise that no man will ever fully understand woman's sexual function or dysfunction," they conclude that a man can "never be secure in his concepts because he can never experience orgasm as a woman."[18]

It is foolish to assert that this claim rests on laboratory experimentation. Actually, we have heard the same argument before—from blacks claiming that whites cannot understand them, and from women claiming that men cannot understand them. In each case, the claim is a consequence of a conflict, of a struggle for power, and we should recognize it as such. But Masters and Johnson assert this claim as if it were a scientific fact, which they then deploy to justify their use of therapy teams and their bias against individ-

‡ I am borrowing the concept of base rhetoric from Richard Weaver, who identifies it as that language which seeks to move us toward evil by "always trying to keep its objects from the support which personal courage, noble associations, and divine philosophy provide a man."[17] His paradigm of base rhetoric is political propaganda.

ual therapists. Of course, no man can experience a
woman's orgasm. But neither can a woman experience
a man's orgasm—or even another woman's. Moreover,
Masters and Johnson pay only lip service to this princi-
ple. Although they are a heterosexual couple, they treat
dysfunctional homosexuals instead of insisting, as their
theory requires, that such persons be treated by a homosexual therapy team.

Masters and Johnson love authority, especially medical authority, and most of all their own. Having rejected patient self-selection as a legitimate criterion for
acceptance in their program, and having proved to
themselves that "a history of at least six months of
prior psychotherapeutic failure to remove the symptoms of sexual dysfunction [is] a poorly contrived
standard, of little screening value," Masters and Johnson solve the problem of patient selection by delegat-
ing the responsibility for it to authority: "A reasonably
effective method of screening [requires] that no patients be accepted at the Foundation unless they have
been referred from authority."[19] (This self-imposed
rule is, however, still another fraud: Masters and Johnson have not adhered to it in screening homosexual clients.) Masters and Johnson imply that they do not accept or reject patients; only the Foundation does.
Moreover, the patients are not referred *by an authority;* they are referred *from authority.* Who is authority?
"As authority, the Foundation accepts physicians, psychologists, social workers, and theologians."[20] An interesting list. Social workers and theologians are authorities on the problems of "marital units"; ethicists

and sociologists are not; physicians are, but philosophers are not. Conspicuous by their absence from the authorities are lawyers, legislators, judges, writers—and wise men and women.

Inevitably, Masters and Johnson's anti-individualistic bias—in particular, their linking sexual performance to marriage—catches up with them. Actually, erotic pleasure and marriage have little to do with one another. Marriage may facilitate or hinder sexual relations between the partners. As a social institution, it shapes our sexual performances and erotic pleasures, just as religious laws and social customs shape our diets and culinary pleasures. But it makes no more sense to insist that a young woman who does not enjoy sex (and who may therefore be diagnosed as orgasmically dysfunctional) be treated only in conjunction with her husband —than that a young woman who does not enjoy food (and who may therefore be diagnosed as having anorexia nervosa) be treated only in conjunction with her mother or father.

Yet, not only do Masters and Johnson insist on such a therapeutic arrangement, they also insist that individuals with sexual dysfunctions who have no partners acquire a partner for the purpose of therapy. This is a trap of their own making. They insist on treating only units. Were they willing to treat men and women as individuals, they would have no reason to refuse individual treatment to married men and women who wish to avoid their mates—in bed as well as in therapy. Ostensibly, their problem was "the demand to develop a psychosocial rationale for therapeutic control of unmarried men and women that might be referred for treatment."[21] From this definition of the problem they swiftly move to the following solution for it—"the obvious clinical demand for a female partner."[22] This is simply not true. The demand for such a partner was not clinical but personal—originating from Masters and Johnson's decisions about how to intervene in the lives of certain individuals.

Obviously, when a man and woman are married, they influence each other's behavior, including sexual behavior. Hence, it is possible to counsel them either as members of a pair or as individuals. But when an unmarried person—unattached to a member of the other sex (or the same sex)—seeks help for sexual problems, there is no sexual pair or unit. To bring one into being, to manufacture a sexual pair for the sole purpose of treatment, is quite different from recognizing the reality of a pair existing prior to, and independently of, the proposed cure.

Asserting, as an undisputable fact, that there is a "clinical demand for the female partner," Masters and Johnson explain that such a partner is needed

> . . . to share the patient's concerns for successful treatment, to cooperate in developing physically the suggestions presented during the sessions in therapy, and most important, to exemplify for the male various levels of female responsivity. . . . In brief, someone to hold on to, talk to, work with, learn from, be a part of, and above all else, *give to* and *get from* during the sexually dysfunctional male's two weeks in the acute phase of therapy.[23]

At no point in this passage do Masters and Johnson

acknowledge that what the female partner is for is to have sexual intercourse with the male patient. Although Masters and Johnson act, talk, and write as if they were concerned with sexual pleasure, and although they have made money from their work, they consistently deny having any interest in sexual pleasure or money. For example, on the book jacket of *Human Sexual Response,* the only aims Masters and Johnson acknowledge are helping "mates" to achieve "sexual adjustment" (which is a far cry from sexual pleasure) and helping the profession of "medicine [to] assume responsibility" for the sex education of its own members (which is a far cry from liberating men and women from the shackles of sexual misinformation or inhibition).[24] But these claims are false. Sexual pleasure is no more reducible to sexual physiology than is pleasure in listening to music reducible to auditory physiology. The longer Masters and Johnson posture as medical scientists, the more they give themselves away as the naive moralizers they are. Their most recent book, on homosexuality, is embarrassingly self-revealing—and utterly self-destructive of their claim to being value-free scientists of sex.

In April 1979, the Masters and Johnson study on homosexuality was released with the same hoopla that characterized their previous announcements of therapeutic breakthroughs against the dread diseases of human sexuality. This time Masters and Johnson told the press—before copies of *Homosexuality in Perspective*[25] or even galleys of it were available for review—that homosexuality was not a disease but that nonethe-

less they could usually cure it in two weeks. Despite
the ridiculous inconsistency inherent in that dual claim,
Time, Newsweek, and the New York *Times* were en-
thusiastic about the latest Masters and Johnson discoveries. "The entire orgasmic experience [of heterosexuals and homosexuals] is indistinguishable,"
explained Masters to *Time* magazine.[26] Armed with
that conflation of physiology and ethics, *Time* approv-
ingly concluded that "the researchers believe that their
demonstration of 'nearly identical response vectors' will
gradually lead to more public acceptance of homosexuality."[27] Although Masters and Johnson now plead for
the approval of homosexuality, *Time* continues to char-
acterize their approach as having a "narrow focus on
biology" which has helped to give people "a sense of
legitimacy about sex" that they never had before.[28] In
Homosexuality in Perspective, Masters and Johnson actually assert that "Now that it has been established
that homosexual men and women are not physiologically different, it is also reasonable to speculate that in
the near future, a significant measure of the current
onus of public opprobrium will be eased from the men
and women with homosexual preference."[29]

I disagree. For those who regard homosexuality as
sinful—for example, because of the Judeo-Christian
religious teaching on the subject—Masters and Johnson's physiological argument for equality between heterosexuals and homosexuals must appear sophomoric.
Suppose that a gastrointestinal physiologist were to
claim (as indeed he might, with veracity) that because
the gastric juices secreted in response to beef, pork,
and human flesh are identical—eating pork is not sinful

for Orthodox Jews, and eating human flesh is not sinful for anyone. I am not arguing, of course, that homosexual acts are sinful. I am arguing that their sinfulness or nonsinfulness cannot depend on the physiology of orgasms in homosexuals.

The basic thesis Masters and Johnson advance in *Homosexuality in Perspective* is similar to the one they advanced in their earlier volumes. In each case they propose to rehabilitate "sexual underdogs"—women and homosexuals—by claiming that they are sexually superior. Previously they claimed that women were more "sexy" than men; now they claim that homosexuals are more "sexy" than heterosexuals. " 'Heterosexual partnership,' they told *Medical World News*, 'is handicapped by cultural pressures on heterosexuals to regard coitus as the be-all and end-all of sex.' . . . In short, homosexual couples had more fun."[30]

This is depressingly familiar. Masters and Johnson's research is merely a variation on the theme that the oppressed are morally superior.[31] To the special virtuousness of the poor, the special spirituality of the Negro, and the special authenticity of the mad, they have now added the special sexual prowess of the woman and the special sexual sensitivity of the homosexual. The sexual superiority of homosexuals has, indeed, become an integral part of the sexual revisionist doctrine. For example, William Simon, a senior sociologist at the University of Indiana's Institute for Sex Research, says that he pities the man "who's trapped into heterosexual monogamy. . . . Men who are exclusively homosexual . . . can engage in sexual activity from many more angles, playing many more roles."[32] Thus do the oppressed first become the oppressor's equals and then his superiors—all in the name of science.

Masters and Johnson's comparison of homosexual and heterosexual acts is of a piece with their comparison of autoerotic and heteroerotic acts. In each case, they view sex mechanically, on the model of urination or defecation, as a mechanism for the relief of tension. That explains why they think that masturbation produces better orgasms than intercourse. What, indeed, could be more revealing of their idea of lovemaking than their reference to the self-stimulated male sex organ as the "penis unencumbered by vaginal containment,"[33] or their reference to the ecstasies of the masturbating woman unhindered by "the psychic distractions of a coital partner."[34] What Masters and Johnson forget is that, after nursing, sex is the most basic social arrangement for satisfying the pervasive and powerful human hunger for being needed/wanted and loved/satisfied. That experience—called love and celebrated in the poetry and prose of all peoples throughout human history—so transcends the physiological need for tension-relief that it can be spiritually satisfying even in the absence of providing relief of sexual tension. But love is a profoundly personal experience and hence completely foreign to Masters and Johnson's vocabulary and habits of thought.

Homosexuality in Perspective is a heavily padded and horribly written book. But it offers further revelations about Masters and Johnson's work. For example, Masters and Johnson acknowledge that they have provided sexual partners—both male and female and for both heterosexual and homosexual acts—for individuals they call uncommitted.[35] They describe this activity by using terms such as "assigned partner," "assigned couple," and "paired." To some lucky uncommitted persons, Masters and Johnson assigned more than one partner: "Two uncommitted women interacted with 2 different assigned partners, forming 4 assigned couples."[36] Masters and Johnson's use of the verb "interacted" is, of course, a code word for the most direct and impersonal sexual acts possible. Moreover, Masters and Johnson are now just as proud about procuring homosexual partners for "experimental singles" as they had been earlier about refusing to procure heterosexual partners for sexually dysfunctional women.

One of the most interesting aspects of their report on homosexuality is the insight it affords into the sorts of persons they sought out and selected as assigned partners: "None of the 10 homosexual men reported a homosexual or heterosexual relationship that lasted more than three months, nor did they express interest in any long-term commitment. According to their description, they interacted with partners primarily for sexual satisfaction."[37] The individuals so selected displayed impressive sexual readiness with unknown partners, which is hardly surprising.*

In this connection Masters and Johnson emphasize

* "Homosexual study subjects usually required considerably less acclimation opportunity compared to heterosexuals of similar age groups and educational backgrounds. For example, of the 16 assigned homosexual partners, only 6 requested time spent in laboratory acclimation. Of the 14 assigned heterosexual subjects (study group A), 9 required orientation procedures. . . ."[38]

that the participants in their research on homosexuality
had nothing to fear—because the sexual partners they
procured for them were guaranteed pure: "Assigned
subjects voiced occasional concern about the risk of
contracting venereal disease via their laboratory exposure, but this concern was minimized by use of appropriate screening procedures."[39]

What was the point of fourteen years of such research? What did Masters and Johnson find out? Nothing that hasn't been known before. By their own admission, they have only proved their own premise about
homosexuality—that "homosexuality and heterosexuality have far more similarities than differences."[40]
This is like rediscovering the wheel. Why, then, are
Masters and Johnson so entranced with this finding?
Because, although they disclaim any moral or political
interests, they are, even at this late date, trying to com-
bat old-fashioned religious prejudices against certain
sex acts by means of "scientific" evidence: "The general public as well as many segments of the scientific
community remain convinced that there are marked
functional disparities between homosexual and heterosexual men and women. This cultural precept was
originally initiated and has been massively supported
by theologic doctrine."[41] Yet, Masters and Johnson
claim that their book should not be interpreted as taking a social, legal, or religious position.[42]

All the insincerity and inconsistency that Masters
and Johnson have produced about sex and sex therapy
pale by comparison with their views on the therapy of
homosexuality. Homosexuality, they assert, is not a disease. This does not stop them from using the term "pa-

tient" to identify the homosexual person who supposedly wants to become heterosexual or from using the term "treatment" to describe their own efforts to help him behave heterosexually.

What is Masters and Johnson's real moral position on homosexuality? Do they support or oppose true legal and personal nondiscrimination against homosexuals? Actually, as Paul Robinson noted several years before the publication of *Homosexuality in Perspective,* Masters and Johnson are decidedly anti-homosexual.[43] The evidence for this is abundant. For example, when homosexual men who are married to conceal their true sexual preference present themselves for therapy, they are never advised to try to accept their homosexual inclination and seek self-esteem as dignified and competent individuals whose moral worth does not depend on their sexual orientation. On the contrary, Masters and Johnson make the same effort to help these men function heterosexually as they do for those whose problems are unrelated to homosexuality.

Masters and Johnson thus ignore that a socially accredited heterosexual commitment may serve as a convenient cover, enabling men and women to engage in homosexual practices more safely than they could without it. Today, heterosexuality is like a majority religion (say, Christianity), homosexuality is like a minority religion persecuted by the majority (say, Judaism), and the married homosexual is like the Jew seemingly converted to Catholicism (say, in fifteenth-century Spain, where they were called Marranos—or Judaizers, if they were suspected of practicing Judaism in secret). Furthermore, while heterosexual or homosexual preference may represent the result of both learning and biological predisposition—the preference for various religious practices is clearly the result of nothing but learning! This analogy—between sexual and religious preferences and practices—throws into bold relief Masters and Johnson's naive, but nonetheless pernicious, anti-homosexual prejudice.

That prejudice surfaced again when, on October 1, 1978, while attending a seminar at Stanford University, Masters and Johnson were interviewed by a reporter for the San Francisco *Examiner*. "Homosexuality," explained Masters, "is a natural expression of sexuality."[44] The reporter then asked Masters and Johnson their opinion about Proposition 6, on which the people of California were to vote in November (which they subsequently soundly defeated). To the reporter's amazement, "Dr. and Mrs. Masters refused to discuss Proposition 6, the antihomosexual Briggs initiative. 'We're not dodging your questions,' Masters told the *Examiner* before addressing 1,100 persons in the Cabana Hyatt Hotel. 'We just don't feel qualified to answer.'"[45] Recognizing that Proposition 6 was to homosexuality what the early National Socialist laws were to Judaism, it was opposed by the entire political spectrum in California. Nevertheless, Masters refused to say, clearly and plainly, whether he supported or opposed the Briggs initiative.

In short, Masters and Johnson do not oppose sexual (religious) prejudice by appealing to the moral legitimacy of diverse sexual (religious) practices. They oppose it by claiming that the diversity is deceptive, or even nonexisting—concealing a basic similarity between seemingly different practices. Homosexuals are really (physiologically) like heterosexuals! (Catholics are, physiologically, like Protestants; Jews are, physiologically, like Moslems.) Indeed they are. But the plea for accepting a minority because it resembles the majority is, in effect, a denial of the minority's right to be different.

Masters once explained the core concept of his sex therapy to a meeting of the American Psychiatric Association as follows: "What . . . tremendously bothers us today is the fact that not a man or woman in this room has ever had the privilege of living in a culture that accepted sex as a natural function."[46] Saying that our culture does not accept sex as a natural function is, to put it mildly, saying something stupid. No culture does. No culture accepts anything important that people do as simply natural. The Jewish, Christian, and Mohammedan religions—and, indeed, every culture—all offer various prescriptions and proscriptions not only with respect to sex but also with respect to food and drink. In that sense, they do not accept alimentation as a natural function either. Perhaps Masters and Johnson should now devote their efforts toward making eating and drinking natural functions—that is, functions performable under any circumstance and with no regard for anything but the ingestion of digestible materials. If what I am saying here seems obvious, beware—for the very opposite of it seems obvious to Masters: "I've delivered normal baby boys that have had four erections before they took their first gasp. And about three years ago we established that baby girls involuntarily

lubricate in the first four to six hours of life. If one has
an erection or lubricates in the first few hours of life,
there has hardly been a chance to learn how to do
this."[47]

The sexual *reflex* of a newborn baby is one thing; the
sexual *act* of an adult is another. How does Masters go
from the one to the other? He doesn't. It is enough for
him to toss out statements about the wonderful nat-
uralness of infants and to let it go at that: "The capacity to respond," Masters emphasized, "is a congenitally
determined phenomenon—the capacity to ejaculate, the
capacity for orgasm; these facilities we are born
with."[48]

We are indeed born with the facilities for orgasm. If
we did not have an inborn potentiality for orgasm, how
could we have an orgasm? All capacities of this sort are
inborn. For example, we have a capacity for walking
and swimming, but not for flying; hence, we can learn
to walk and to swim, but not to fly. Although sexual capacities are inborn, human beings must learn to engage
in sexual acts and to experience sexual feelings in certain personally and socially acceptable ways. In fact,
Masters and Johnson are engaged in preaching about
certain kinds of sexual behaviors and experiences, but
pretend—as physicians have for centuries—that they are
engaged merely in restoring human beings from an unnatural state of sickness (as if disease were unnatural)
to a natural state of health.†

† "Sex is a natural function," Masters reiterated. "And if it is a
natural function, then we don't need to teach anything; we only need
to remove stumbling blocks."[49] Masters' message is simple and misleading. But it is precisely those qualities, combined with a gnostic vision

In his address to the American Psychiatric Association in 1975, Masters identified three components of his method. One is the concept of "sex as a natural function." Another is "a knowledge of the basic sciences of successful psychotherapy" (whatever that means). And the third is "the realization that there was no such thing as an uninvolved partner."[50]

This last concept is, again, misleadingly characterized. The proposition that every partner is "involved"—that is, is partly responsible for the identified patient's sexual dysfunction—is not a realization but a judgment. And it is, once more, a judgment with the most transparent purpose—namely, to justify the use of dual sex teams and "surrogate wives."[51] Masters' posture toward other people's sexual teamwork is pertinent in this connection. He once modestly suggested that, save for himself and his wife, there are hardly any honest and competent sex therapists in America: "Dr. William Masters said that only one in 100 [sex] clinics or treatment centers in the United States are legitimate. . . . 'The vast majority of the clinics offer little more than a superficial sex education at best and dangerous quackery at worst.' "[52]

Regarding what sex therapists and surrogates may or may not do with their patients, Masters is not merely blind, he is brazen. In an interview in *Time* magazine in 1974, Masters acknowledged that his cures of impotent men were due largely to the efforts of the prostitutes he procured for them: "In 1970 the St. Louis clinic stopped using surrogates. . . . Masters regrets

---

of, and claim for, an infinitely perfectible human sexuality, that invite bracketing Masters with Marx and Freud.

having had to give up the surrogate therapy.‡ . . . 'The
success statistics with single impotent males have completely reversed,' he says. 'We now have a failure rate
of 70% to 75%.' "⁵⁴

This is a remarkable admission on the part of a physician intent on treating patients. Suppose that a physician's treatment of his patients depends on using mor-
phine, performing abortions, or keeping his patient's
communications absolutely confidential; and suppose,
further—a contingency by no means farfetched—that
for reasons beyond his control, the physician was pre-
vented from using these particular methods. Under
such circumstances, it seems that the morally proper
course would be for the physician to declare that he
can no longer practice his particular method of healing,
and hence refuse to accept patients who expect to be
treated by methods previously advertised but currently
unavailable. But this is not what Masters has done. Although he has stopped using surrogates, he has not
publicized that fact as he had publicized using them
(nor, despite his admitted inability to treat impotent
men effectively under such circumstances, has he
stopped accepting such patients for treatment). Instead
of doing any of these things, what Masters has done is
to attack other sex therapists, especially those who still
use surrogates. We are now witnessing Masters calling
his imitators immoral—a case, if ever there was one, of
the pot calling the kettle black.

‡ Masters and Johnson stopped using surrogates "when the husband
of one sued them for alienation of affection and a big settlement was
made out of court."⁵³

4

SEX AS
TREATMENT—
IN PRACTICE

In 1975, the second annual "Hookers Convention" was
held in San Francisco. The conference was attended by
many prominent persons—among them Flo Kennedy,
co-founder of the National Women's Political Caucus,
and Jane Fonda, the actress—who called for the decrim-
inalization of prostitution. As one might expect, the
program included a panel on Prostitution as Therapy,
at which Dr. Jennifer James, an anthropologist at the
University of Washington, revealed that a "six-year
study of prostitution she conducted in Seattle showed
that the practice was harmless and socially beneficial. . . . A prostitute is paid not to reject."[1] Dr.

James claimed that "the rate of venereal disease among prostitutes was lower than among high school students because they're professionals and it would be bad for business to do otherwise."[2] Clearly, Masters and Johnson are latecomers to the game of calling prostitution sex therapy, and sex therapy a profession.

The competition between male medical sex therapists and female nonmedical sex therapists is creating a conflict between them that has all the earmarks of an earlier conflict in which male medical obstetricians fought against and defeated female nonmedical midwives. Today the new sex therapists claim superiority over the old sex therapists in exactly the same way that the (new) obstetricians claimed superiority over the (old) midwives a century ago—that is, by asserting that they are professionals whose practice is based on science and a dedication to protect the public—whereas their lay competitors are quacks whose practice is based on superstition and a desire to exploit the public.

At the moment, the battle lines between these combatants are still rather fluid, both sides scoring victories and suffering defeats. Not only are sex therapists often regarded as practicing a dubious art, but prostitutes are sometimes accorded the status of therapists. For example, in a recent controversy concerning the curative effects of copulation, the contention that prostitution is therapy was upheld by one of the most important agencies of the U.S. government—namely, the Internal Revenue Service. A physician suggested to a man that he engage the services of a prostitute. He did so and deducted his payments to her on his income tax. The deduction was allowed on the condition that he "cooperate with the IRS in their investigation of the prostitute. Result: the man saved $200 in taxes, and the woman was hit with a claim for $90,000 in back taxes."[3]

The West German medical profession and government have also recognized prostitution as a treatment. A physician in Schleswig prescribed weekly visits to a brothel for a young man diagnosed as suffering from excessive sexual excitement. The cost of these visits was paid by the bureau of social services of the city of Flensburg. An investigation of the affair ended with the determination that the prescription conformed to the law, which stated that funds allocated to this agency may be used for "medically prescribed measures for the prevention or removal of a handicap." The agency's files showed that the prostitute gave the patient a receipt each time he visited for "sexual assistance."[4] So much for the old sex therapy.

Masters and Johnson have played a dual role in modern sexology: they have furnished a seemingly new theory of sexuality and legitimized an ostensibly new form of sex therapy. Actually, their theory has served to justify and rationalize their therapy, and their sex therapy has served as evidence of the validity of the theory.

Contemporary sex therapists acknowledge that Masters and Johnson's initial publications were influential partly because they were ideally suited to become the "scientific foundations" for the budding business of the new sex therapy. How very far Masters' real goal lies from offering a science of human sexuality, and lies instead in developing a therapeutic bureaucracy and a

technology for it, is revealed most clearly toward the
end of *Human Sexual Inadequacy*. "A conservative es-
timate," Masters declares, "would indicate half the
marriages [in the United States] are either presently
sexually dysfunctional or imminently so in the future."[5]
The only hope for this sexual-matrimonial disaster lies,
he tells us, in the creation of "a major postgraduate
training program to develop seminar leaders for therapy training centers throughout the country."[6]

Within two years after the publication of Masters
and Johnson's *Human Sexual Inadequacy* in 1970, five
sex therapy clinics opened in New York, and by 1973
seven more hospital-related sex clinics began to operate
in the greater New York area.[7] Concerning the economics of these clinics, Joseph LoPiccolo noted that, in
the United States, "the average cost range for fifteen
hours of outpatient psychotherapy with a private practice psychologist or psychiatrist is between $300 and
$750. Yet the average cost range for fifteen hours (the
usual duration) of sex therapy from one of the many
sex therapy centers is between $2,500 and $4,000."[8]
However, this is not so remarkable if we remember
that psychotherapists sell conversation, whereas many
sex therapists sell sex.

The use of surrogates is central to the new sex therapies. In fact, Masters and his acolytes have successfully
deployed this euphemism to mask a full-fledged sexual
con game. Linda Wolfe, who wrote a well-researched
story on the use of surrogates in sex therapy, relates
that she has "spoken to several practitioners here [New
York] who admit to using surrogates—usually call

girls who charge $100 a night—but they will not let me
interview the call girls/surrogates. Nor do they want
their own names mentioned."[9] Wolfe also talked to surrogates, both in New York and California. One of them,
who is identified pseudonymously as "Pandora," regards herself as both a surrogate and a therapist:

> Pandora takes her referrals from various physicians
> and psychiatrists around town. She started out charg-
> ing $500 for a set of twelve sessions, spread over a
> fourteen-day period, three to four hours the session.
> She has just raised her fee to $750 and has found no
> decrease in the demand for her services. She has had,
> she reports, 100% success.[10]

In California Wolfe talked to several women, two of
whom act as both therapist and surrogate at a clinic
called the Berkeley Group for Sexual Development.[11]
She found the surrogates to be sincere, "viewing themselves as dedicated, as bent on service to mankind—in
the old-fashioned sense of the expression."[12] One of the
surrogate-therapists mentioned by Wolfe was identified
in *Newsweek* in 1972 (the year before Wolfe's article
was published) as follows: "An attractive brunette of
26 who intends to become an occupational therapist is
earning her way through San Jose State University by
working as a sexual therapist. She charges $50 for a
two-and-a-half hour session—including love-making—in
her sensuously decorated apartment with its incense
burner and heated water bed."[13] This woman's success
seems to have made some of her colleagues envious, for
one of them accused her, to Wolfe, of exhibiting excessive therapeutic zeal by means of "her frequent or-

gasms with her male patients ('She gives them to the male like gifts')."[14]

The new sex therapy quickly caught on in England too. Martin Cole, a Ph.D. in plant genetics, directs the Institute for Sex Research in Birmingham, England, where "the No. 1 teacher . . . is his 25-year-old third wife Barbara." Barbara Cole and other volunteers, male and female, are said to teach men and women patients how to copulate successfully. After having logged up no fewer than fifty therapeutic acts of coitus, Mrs. Cole declared: "When a man of this kind, tortured and desperately unhappy, is at last able to make successful love with me, the feeling for both of us is tremendous."[15] Dr. Cole claimed (in 1973) that "One in ten British men needs help with his sex life," and that "I could keep 50 therapists busy if I had them."[16]

Six years later, Cole's business was booming. According to a report in the *Guardian,* he was employing twenty female "surrogates," at least one of whom was a former prostitute: "Before she [Dawn] started to work for the Institute she was employed in a sauna giving what is described as 'hand relief' and sometimes having intercourse with clients. Although she earns less as a surrogate, she is happy to be free of the constant fear of a police raid and bad publicity."[17] The financial success of Cole's operation is no doubt helped also by the fact that the British taxpayer is paying for the surrogates' services: "The fees of some patients are met from NHS or probation service funds and Dr. Cole thinks it is likely that the payments are probably ac-

counted for by the referring agency in terms which dis-
guise the fact that the patient is receiving surrogate
therapy."[18]

Naturally, this sort of thing is upsetting the doctors.
They complain that their nonmedical competitors are
quacks and demand "some kind of licensing procedure
to govern sex therapy."[19] So it behooves us to famil-
iarize ourselves not only with what medical sex therapists say they do, but also with what they do.

Thanks to the First Amendment and the enterprise
of American writers and publishers, we can learn about
the new sex therapy from the surrogates themselves.
My following remarks are based on the information
contained in a paperback volume entitled *Surrogate
Wife,* by "Valerie X. Scott" and Herbert d'H. Lee. On
the front cover, the book is described as "The story of a
Masters and Johnson sexual therapist and the nine
cases she treated." The text on the back cover reads:

> "Valerie X. Scott" is not the therapist's real name. For
> obvious reasons, she prefers to keep that private.
>
> Valerie was employed by the Masters and Johnson
> Research Foundation in St. Louis as an "in-bed" thera-
> pist in the treatment of male sexual inadequacy. The
> nature of this therapy may be shocking to some but has
> proved its value. Valerie was assigned to become an
> actual sexual partner for the unhappy, sometimes de-
> spairing men who came to Masters and Johnson seek-
> ing a cure for impotence. Valerie's co-author was one
> of her patients. . . . Here, in her own astonishingly
> frank language, is Valerie's vivid descriptions of her
> nine "cures"—the techniques she used, how they were
> adapted to the very different kinds of men she helped,

and her reactions as a woman to her role as surrogate
wife.* [20]

Herbert Lee—whom, in keeping with his own style, I
shall call Herbert—is a professional writer. He claims to
have made the pilgrimage to St. Louis in search of his
potency. But the Foundation, Herbert notes, was originally set up to assist only couples. Accordingly, female
surrogates were supplied to men (but no male surrogates were supplied to women). Up to the time when
Herbert arrived for treatment (the date is not given),
"thirteen women were accepted as surrogate wives
from among thirty-one volunteers."[22] Their relationship
to Masters and Johnson is described as follows: "Once
assigned a patient, the surrogate was given a complete
dossier of his life and psycho-sexual background, and
then the details of his specific problem. From there on,
she checked in day by day, receiving instructions from
either Dr. Masters or Mrs. Johnson, and also reporting
on the time spent with the patient."[23] The surrogates
also received money from Masters and Johnson.

Since the Foundation offered help only to couples,
Herbert expected to be assigned a surrogate. He describes his first impression of her as follows:

> I was sitting beside a girl who was now revealed to me
> as a lovely redhead of perhaps twenty-six with long
> legs showing to mid-thigh under her tan mini and
> open short coat; a girl whose bust swelled dramati-

---

* The authenticity of this report, at least so far as the attributions
to Masters and Johnson go, is supported by the authors' acknowledg-
ment in the Foreword. They write: "All personal names in *Surrogate
Wife* (including our own) have been changed except for those of
Dr. Masters and Mrs. Johnson."[21]

cally; a girl whose face and body made me want her immediately. A girl who belonged to me; whom I had in effect purchased at the clinic two days ago; who would be mine in every way that a man wants a desirable woman.[24]

William Masters is a doctor who treats patients. Patients, one assumes, are sick. Was Herbert sick? After his initial workup, he was interviewed by Masters, who told him that "his [Masters'] examination and the lab results had convinced him that there was absolutely nothing wrong with me."[25] Clearly, Herbert was an ideal patient for the healer whose passion is to denounce his competitors as quacks. Immediately, Herbert felt better: "I believed him. . . . It was as if one could be analyzed by Freud, at the time when Freud was considered the one and only source of help, the unchallenged master in his field."[26]

Masters lost no time in starting the therapy. "Dr. Masters said that tonight Valerie would come to my suite. We could have dinner in or out, a drink or two, and we would then undress and go to bed—not to engage in sexual intercourse, but to explore each other, to play, to touch, to reestablish my sense of sexual pleasure."[27]

At this point in the book, the narrative shifts to Valerie's story, in which Herbert's case is reduced to a single episode. After some information about Valerie's personal background, we learn how she became a surrogate:

My job provided just the barest essentials, after Mother's nursing bills, and anything extra was always

welcome. There, it's something I dreaded saying!
Money was the most important reason, at least initially, though Dr. Masters and Mrs. Johnson didn't
know it. . . . Bill and Gini were terribly selective in
choosing surrogates, and I felt their accepting me was
real kudos. But at that time, when I'd agreed to join
the program and was sitting in Gini's office, it was the
desperate need for immediate money that decided the
issue.[28]

In return for the money Masters gave Valerie, what
did he expect her to do? Here is her understanding of
the bargain: "I know, from my discussions at the Foundation, that I'd eventually have to use every means at
my disposal to give this man erections and orgasms.
That was the name of the game—to prove to him that
he was capable with me, and therefore with his wife
and any other woman."[29] The man to whom Valerie
here refers was married, but preferred to be treated
with a surrogate wife rather than with his real wife. In
this case, then, Masters and Johnson were not only procuring a sexual partner for a man but were also participating in the planning and consummation of an adulterous relationship.

The similarities between old-fashioned prostitution
and new-fashioned sex therapy have been noted by a
number of observers from a variety of disciplines, including the law.

Masters began his sex research by using professional
prostitutes, a practice which, in the face of public criticism, he soon abandoned. To replace the prostitutes,
Masters began to recruit volunteers through the Wash-

SEX AS TREATMENT—IN PRACTICE

ington University academic community. Although
Masters tried to conceal his actual deeds behind a
semantic smokescreen of medical terms and the rit-
ualized incantation of the sacred words "couples" and
"marital units," the publication of *Human Sexual Inadequacy* revealed that "fifty-four single men and three
unmarried women had participated in the human sexual dysfunction treatment over an eleven-year period."[30] Sixteen of the single men and all of the unmarried women brought their own sexual companions with
them. Masters and Johnson called these paramours "re-
placement partners" and insisted on treating them as
members of the couple. In a legal analysis of the new
sex therapy, David Leroy observes that Masters and
Johnson did not report what effort, if any, they made to
determine "whether either the patient or the replace-
ment partner was married to another person at the
time of treatment," thus implicating themselves in a
legally adulterous situation.[31] However, this legal problem pales in comparison to the problem generated by
Masters and Johnson's use of surrogates. In this connection too, Masters and Johnson dissemble and deceive—and not just by using mendacious euphemisms
for describing the women paid to have intercourse with
men.† Although they claim that the function of the sur-

† My critical remarks about Masters and Johnson's potential law
violations, incurred as a result of their researching and practicing "sex
therapy," do not imply that I approve of the laws they might have
violated. On the contrary, I consider all laws restricting contractual
relations between consenting adults odious (the exceptions being "con-
tracts" for the enslavement or killing of one of the parties). However,
since Masters and Johnson believe that the state should play an active
role promoting "scientific sex therapy" and prohibiting "sex-therapeutic

rogate is to stand in for the man's wife or private para-
mour, in fact they treat the man-and-his-surrogate couple quite differently from the man-and-his-wife couple
(or the man-and-his-private-paramour couple). The
nonsurrogate-couple is treated as a unit, both individuals being regarded as patients, both meeting with
Masters and Johnson in a four-way therapeutic interview. With the surrogate-couple, however, Masters and
Johnson modify their procedure, excluding the surrogate from the professional consultations. Instead, she
reports, usually to Mrs. Johnson, after each session, and
receives instructions on how and how far to proceed in
the next meeting.[32] The surrogates were paid for their
sexual services, the fee per patient going as high as
$250.[33]

Since the surrogates were paid for sexual services,
and since the single men who came for treatment knew
that they would be provided with sexual partners,
Leroy believes that "all or most of the participants so
involved may have committed offenses related to laws
against prostitution."[34] Why, then, was Masters never
so prosecuted? The major reason is "the careful culti-
vation of favorable public opinion by Dr. Masters' un-
disputably 'medical' program, attached to a major university, which was selectively revealed in gradual
stages with an appropriately 'moral' husband and wife
focus, in a book purged of all prurient appeal by deliberately technical language."[35]

Not only are the surrogates themselves potential law

charlatanism" (and prostitution), a critical examination of the present
legal status of the Masters and Johnson type of sex therapy seems to
me both justified and relevant.

violators, but so are the therapists. A person who places a woman into the trade of prostitution, employs and transports her, or otherwise supervises her career may be considered to be violating the pandering and procuring statutes.[36] Nor does the chain of criminal activity connected with this type of therapy stop there. The clinic itself may be considered "a potential pimping defendant," while those who refer patients to the Foundation (the patient's own physician, minister, or social worker) may be guilty of soliciting and encouraging prostitution.[37]

Ignorant of their own historical roots, modern sexologists advocate not only intercourse but also masturbation as treatments—as if the ostensibly therapeutic use of these sexual acts constituted novel medical discoveries. But the new sex therapists have only poured old wine into new skins, repackaging sexual arousal, stimulation, and gratification as specific therapeutic techniques.

Actually, the famous Greek physician Galen of Pergamon (A.D. 129–199) recommended masturbation—administered by the doctor to the patient—for the relief of "hysteria": "Following the warmth of the remedies and arising from the touch of the genital required by the treatment, there followed twitchings accompanied at the same time by pain and pleasure after which she emitted turbid and abundant sperm [i.e., genital secretions]. From that time on she was freed of all the evil she felt."[38]

Toward the end of the nineteenth century—when the belief that masturbation caused illness, or was itself an

illness, reached its zenith—Mark Twain ridiculed that
notion by presciently satirizing its therapeutic powers:

> Homer in the second book of the Iliad, says with fine
> enthusiasm, "Give me masturbation or give me death!"
> Caesar, in his *Commentaries*, says, "To the lonely it is
> company; to the forsaken it is a friend; to the aged and
> to the impotent it is a benefactor; they that are penny-
> less are yet rich, in that they still have this majestic
> diversion." In another place this experienced observer
> has said, "There are times when I prefer it to sodomy."
> Robinson Crusoe says, "I cannot describe what I owe
> to this gentle art." Queen Elizabeth said, "It is the
> bulwark of Virginity." Cetewayo, the Zulu hero, re-
> marked, "A jerk in the hand is worth two in the bush."
> The immortal Franklin has said, "Masturbation is the
> mother of invention." He also said, "Masturbation is the
> best policy." Michelangelo and all the other old
> masters—Old Masters, I will remark, is an abbreviation,
> a contraction—have used similar language. Michelan-
> gelo said to Pope Julius II, "Self-negation is noble, self-
> culture is beneficent, self-possession is manly, but to
> the truly grand and inspiring soul they are poor and
> tame compared to self-abuse."‡ [39]

Mark Twain was jesting. The new sex therapists are,
however, in deadly earnest.

Masters and Johnson promote masturbation because
they think it is therapeutic—maritally as well as medically. Maritally, they claim, masturbation is indicated

‡ The passage cited is from an address Mark Twain delivered to the
"Stomach Club" in Paris in 1879. It was considered so scandalous that
it was not published until eighty-five years later.

for fully half of the husbands and wives in America
whose sexual incompetence threatens their marital bliss
and hence the political stability of the nation itself.[40]
Medically, it is indicated especially for women and for
old men. Women need to masturbate because during
menstruation it "increased the rate of flow, reduced
pelvic cramping when present, and frequently relieved
menstrually associated backaches."[41] It sounds better
than Excedrin. Old men need to masturbate to keep in
shape sexually. Heeding the old saw "Use it, or lose it,"
Masters and Johnson prescribe a kind of penile jogging.

Just how literally and humorlessly Masters and Johnson accept and embrace the doctrine of masturbatory
therapy is exemplified by their discovery of a new sexological disease called masturbatory orgasmic inadequacy.

What is masturbatory orgasmic inadequacy? To its
discoverers, it is, first of all, a bona fide disease:
Masters and Johnson discuss its etiology—usually religion; they identify its incidence—it affects (as we
might expect) only women; and they report their treatment of eleven patients who suffered from this disease
—ten of whom they cured. Their definition of this so-
called pathological condition shows what these moun-
tebanks of masturbation have been able to put over on
an ever-corrupt medical profession and an ever-gullible
public: "A woman with masturbatory orgasmic inadequacy has not achieved orgasmic release by partner or
self-stimulation in either homosexual or heterosexual
experience. She can and does reach orgasmic expression during coital connection."[42]

Consider the indignity implicit in this diagnosis. Re-

gardless of the human situation in which a woman
achieves orgasm by noncoital activity (heterosexual,
homosexual, or solitary, loving or loveless, etc.), and regardless of the means by which she does so (fingers,
dildo, vibrator, water, etc.), Masters and Johnson regard such orgasm as evidence of masturbatory orgasmic adequacy. This is their medical euphemism for
healthy, normal, good. It leads them to conclude that
women who achieve orgasm in heterosexual coitus but
not in masturbating are suffering from masturbatory
orgasmic inadequacy, which is their medical euphemism for sick, abnormal, bad.

The discovery of this disease is an inversion of the
old doctrine of masturbatory insanity. In the nineteenth century, masturbating was an illness and not
masturbating was a treatment; today, not masturbating
is a disease and masturbating is a treatment.

The currently popular methods for teaching masturbation as a treatment, especially to women, are all cut
from the same cloth. The method developed by Charles
Lobitz and Joseph LoPiccolo, two University of Ore-
gon psychologists, is typical and is often cited as a
model. It consists of a series of autoerotic exercises
which they call a nine-step masturbation program.[43]
Among the tasks that Lobitz and LoPiccolo assign to
women are examining the genitals in a mirror, explor-
ing them manually, and identifying pleasurable areas.
A female therapist then teaches the client "techniques
of masturbation including the use of a lubricant." A vibrator may be recommended. After the client "has
achieved orgasm through masturbation, we introduce

the husband to the procedure by having him observe her." The husband is then instructed to masturbate his wife. Finally, "we instruct the couple to engage in intercourse while the husband stimulates his wife's genitals, either manually or with a vibrator."[44] In short, the client is treated like a stupid child taught to perform a particular act by a knowledgeable parent or teacher. Significantly, the ultimate goal of the masturbation program is not that the patient should enjoy sexual self-stimulation, but that she should enter into conjugal masturbatory activity. (The authors always call the male partner the "husband.")

Similar methods are advocated by other sex therapists. For example, Jack Annon, a psychologist at the Sex Counseling Service of the University of Hawaii Medical School, asserts that "self-stimulation ranks first as the most successful way of experiencing orgasm, and 75% of the women who do use this method on a regular basis report that they achieve orgasm within 4 minutes—if they choose to."[45] The caveat—that women can have orgasms with masturbation "if they choose to"—reveals the stupidity of this type of sexological writing. Of course, people can enjoy sex if they want to—just as they can enjoy eating, drinking, smoking, or using drugs if they want to. And if they want to enjoy such activities, then they can teach themselves, or can be taught by friends and lovers, how to do so. Why, then, all the fuss about sex therapists teaching women how to masturbate? Could this be still another variation on the ageless theme of men putting down women?

This suspicion is supported by the fact that much of the current pro-masturbatory literature reflects the

premise that the female genital is a kind of household
appliance whose owner has not understood the instruction manual. The experts must explain to women how
their sexual organs are constructed and how they work
best. Niels Lauersen and Steven Whitney, the authors
of *It's Your Body: A Woman's Guide to Gynecology*,
thus state that because "the clitoris is in a rather incon-
venient position for intercourse,"[46] the female body is
not well made for coitus. But it responds perfectly to
masturbation. It may take considerable effort to make
the machine work, but Lauersen and Whitney reassure
the reader that all it takes is practice and perseverance:
"Initially, she may have to masturbate an hour a day
for several weeks before reaching orgasm. . . . If manual masturbation becomes too strenuous, a vibrator can
certainly help."[47]

The legitimacy of masturbation and the vibrator as
therapeutic techniques in contemporary American medicine is reflected in the following exchange in the
Questions and Answers column of the *Journal of the
American Medical Association*. A physician inquires
about "the value of a vibrator for a healthy woman
who has difficulty achieving orgasm through normal
sexual intercourse." The consultant, William Masters,
replies:

> There is a specific value for the vibrator. If this woman
> has never had an orgasmic experience, regardless of
> stimulative approach, there is a merit in relieving her
> fear that she is incapable of such a response. The
> threat in such a therapeutic technique is that the vi-
> brator can be habituating. It should be used only

within the context of an adequate therapy opportunity to reverse the basic orgasmic dysfunction.[48]

Masters takes it for granted that masturbation is a treatment. By adding that the vibrator "can be habituating [and] should be used only within the context of an adequate therapy opportunity," he implies that, like addictive drugs, vibrators should be available only to patients, perhaps only by prescription.*

The therapeutic powers of masturbation are now propounded with the same smug professional conviction with which its pathogenic powers had been propounded in the past. Because the anti-masturbators wanted to make the practice appear wicked, they called it self-abuse; because the pro-masturbators want to make it appear virtuous, they call it self-pleasuring. The historical parallel between the old and the new medical posture toward masturbation is displayed also in the ways in which the pro-masturbation arguments continue to conform to the ethic and logic of the pro-intercourse arguments they displaced. Formerly the promise of procreation justified intercourse; now the promise of orgasmic intercourse justifies masturba-

* Much of what goes on in the name of sex therapy is morally obtuse. Some of it—like the program at the Loyola University Sexual Dysfunction Clinic in Maywood (a Chicago suburb)—is morally grotesque. The approach of this clinic is claimed to "reflect the philosophy of the Catholic university of which it is a part." However, the program is based on the Masters and Johnson model and includes a "sexological examination" of the wife in the presence of the husband, during which "both husband and wife are encouraged to feel her clitoris." The cost of the treatment "is covered by most insurance plans, Medicare, and public assistance."[49] Someone ought to sue for Medicaid coverage as well.

tion. Even the most radical pro-masturbators fall back
on this justification[50]—which raises a question: Why
should anyone still try to justify masturbation instead
of asserting that it is no one's business but the masturbator's—or nonmasturbator's? If women have a right to
their bodies (as the advocates of therapeutic masturbation maintain), then they need no further justification for sexual acts with consenting adults or with
themselves.

By affirming women's rights to their own bodies, and
yet justifying masturbation as therapy, modern sexologists betray their basic unfamiliarity with the idea of
liberty. For example, Martin Weisberg and Bobbie
Whitney, a male-female team of sex experts, declare:
"Masturbation is important as a therapeutic tool because it teaches the concept of self-pleasuring in its
broadest sense. Once a woman has become reliably
orgasmic from self-stimulation, she can begin to
transfer this responsiveness to her partner relationship."[51] But if what the new sex therapists teach is
self-pleasuring, why don't they teach people how to
drink and smoke and take drugs? Surely, those acts too
are tools for self-pleasuring.

SIECUS—the Sex Information and Education Council of the United States†—has taken an official position
on masturbation. It supports it because it is "natural."[52]
But what human behavior isn't? Belching and farting,
theft and murder, are all natural. Does that make them
desirable or therapeutic? Moreover, although SIECUS

† The roles of SIECUS and Mary Calderone in sex education are
presented in Chapter 7.

correctly connects masturbation with the affirmation of
self-ownership, the concept of self-ownership—which
also entails the right to gamble, take drugs, commit suicide, and other basic libertarian principles—is anath-
ema to SIECUS's liberal supporters.

The assumption that modern sexologists do not understand the concept of self-ownership, or do not believe in it, is supported by many of their remarks. Here
is a typical one: "It [masturbation] should even be encouraged for individual partners during periods of sep-
aration, illness, when one's individual sexual needs are
not able to be managed completely by their spouses,
etc. I often ask couples to give each other permission
on these occasions."[53] This writer refers to individual
sexual needs as if there could be any other, as if couples—perhaps even groups, nations, or humankind as a
whole—could also have sexual needs. His asking "couples to give each other permission" to masturbate man-
ages to convey, in one brief sentence, both his con-
tempt for the English language and his attempt to
mandate one particular version of the marriage contract.

Masturbation—like any sexual activity uninjurious to
others—is a matter of private, personal conduct. It
expresses and reflects, as does all behavior, the individual's medical and moral convictions about the nature of
human sexuality and its proper role in his own life. The
fact that a particular act is unpleasant or bad does not
make it a disease; nor does the fact that it is pleasant or
good make it a treatment.

5

SEXUAL SURGERY

Long before people rationalized sexual surgery on medical grounds, they rationalized it on religious grounds. Indeed, the idea that the sexual organs ought to be surgically altered runs through all of history. Because the genitals (as well as certain other body parts, especially the face) have symbolic meaning, and because culture rests on symbolic interactions, human beings are easily led to believe that, in their natural state, the sexual organs and powers are not in their proper form and hence ought to be enhanced or diminished by means of artifacts or surgical interventions.* [1]

The earliest historical example of sexual surgery is

* I offer this brief overview of both ancient and modern sexual-surgical practices in the hope that it will help the reader to put the preposterous claims of contemporary sexual pathologists and therapists into a critical perspective.

circumcision. According to the Old Testament, its origin and meaning are as follows:

> And God said unto Abraham . . . That is my covenant,
> which you shall keep between me and you and thy
> seed after thee. Every man child among you shall be
> circumcised. And ye shall circumcise the flesh of your
> foreskin; and it shall be a token of the covenant be-
> twixt me and you. . . . And the uncircumcised man
> child whose flesh of his foreskin is not circumcised,
> that soul shall be cut off from his people; he hath bro-
> ken my covenant.[2]

The Bible thus tells the story of the ancient Israelites making a bargain with their god: the Jews give Jehovah their foreskins, in return for which Jehovah gives them preferred nation status. Mutilation of the penis becomes a badge of identity—the mark, according to the Jews, of their being God's Chosen People. Since subsequently the Christians and the Muslims have also claimed, perhaps even more successfully, that they, and they alone, are God's favorite children, this operation must be deemed a failure.

The ancient Israelites seemed to have been decidedly preoccupied with foreskins—viewing the severed flesh of the penis as a trophy, much as headhunters view the severed head:

> And Saul said, Thus shall ye say to David, the king
> desireth not any dowry, but a hundred foreskins of the
> Philistines. . . . Wherefore David arose and went . . .
> and slew of the Philistines two hundred men; and
> David brought their foreskins, and they gave them in
> full tale to the king, that he might be the king's son in
> law.[3]

Despite this biblical passage, most people—Jews and
non-Jews alike—continue to believe that ritual circumcision is evidence of the ancient Hebrews' sophisticated
concern with genital hygiene.† However, such a view is
inconsistent with the fact that Jewish law requires the
circumcision of dead infants:

> An infant who dies before circumcision, whether
> within the eight days or thereafter, must be circum-
> cised at the grave, in order to remove the foreskin
> which is a disgrace to him. . . . If he was buried with-
> out circumcision, and they [his parents] become aware
> of it immediately, when there is no likelihood that the
> body has already begun to decompose, the grave
> should be opened and the circumcision should be per-
> formed. But if they have become aware of it after
> some days, the grave should not be opened.[5]

If Asclepius is the archetypal physician, then surely
Abraham is the archetypal sex-surgeon. He is well
enough known for having invented and popularized
circumcision. (Actually, circumcision was practiced by
the Egyptians, from whom the Jews had copied it.
Routine post-natal circumcision remains the most
widely performed surgery on American males, despite
the fact that the procedure is hazardous and lacks any
medical justification. If performed on infants under one
year of age, there is significant bleeding in 15 percent

---

† Attributing a hygienic or rational basis to certain Jewish religious
laws has been a practice much favored by modern students of religion
and the social sciences. Such theories are, however, contrary to the
facts. Jewish sexual laws, like Jewish dietary laws, are not a matter
of hygiene but a matter of what is now called racism: for example,
the *kashrut* (dietary laws) prohibits drinking wine prepared or even
touched by a non-Jew.[4]

of circumcisions, and serious bleeding, sometimes requiring transfusion, in 2 percent. One neonatal circumcision in 6,000 results in the death of the infant. About
1,325,000 newborn American males are circumcised annually and about 230 of them die as a result of the operation. The annual cost to the "consumer" of this massive sexual-surgical mayhem is estimated to be around
$54 million.[6])

Abraham is much less well known, however, for having also invented a reversal of this operation—specifically, the transplantation of foreskins from cadavers
onto human beings (in the hereafter):

> In the Hereafter Abraham will sit at the entrance of
> *Gehinnom* [Hell] and will not allow any circumcised
> Israelite to descend into it. As for those who sinned un-
> duly, what does he do to them? He removes the fore-
> skin from children who had died before circumcision,
> places it upon them and sends them down to *Ge-
> hinnom.*[7]

In the Hebrew world view, being circumcised is the
ultimate good, because it signifies *inclusion* in the
tribe; and not being circumcised, or having one's circumcision undone, is the ultimate punishment, because
it signifies *exclusion* from the tribe. (In addition to
Abraham, Jewish angels also performed foreskin trans-
plantations.[8])

A more realistic, and indeed quite nonmythical, un-
doing of circumcision was actually practiced by the ancient Jews. This operation—a sort of plastic repair of
the circumcised penis—was not uncommon in pre-
Christian Greece, where Jewish athletes underwent it
so they could compete—nude, of course—in the stadia.

After the birth of Christianity, the operation assumed a new significance for the Jews who believed in the divinity of Jesus: it enabled them to resymbolize—by "making for themselves new prepuces"[9] (that is, by restoring the integrity of the penis)—their dedication to a new faith. Perhaps Saul considered it, but then took the less painful course of changing his name instead. In any case, he declared the practice unnecessary:

> Let every one lead the life which the Lord has assigned to him, and in which God has called him. This is my rule in all the churches. Was any one at the time of his call circumcised? Let him not seek to remove the marks of circumcision.[10]

Although the Christians gave up circumcision, their attitude toward the penis was decidedly less friendly than that of the Jews had been. Believing that sexual desire was itself an evil, the early Christians were ready to assist their aspirations toward asceticism by means of autocastration. In the Gospel according to Matthew, extravagant praise is heaped upon men who "have made themselves eunuchs for the kingdom of heaven's sake."[11] (Some biblical scholars interpret "eunuch" metaphorically, to mean simply a man who renounces marriage in favor of celibacy.‡)

So much for some early examples of sexual surgery. Let us now skip the next eighteen centuries—replete with such practices as castration, infibulation, clitori-

‡ The themes of self-castration and castration have reemerged in modern psychiatry: if a man cuts off his own penis, psychiatrists call him schizophrenic, but if he can persuade a surgeon to cut it off for him, then they call him a transsexual.[12]

dectomy, and the use of the chastity belt—and turn to
a review of modern sexual surgery.

Throughout the nineteenth century, the most common and most feared sexual disease was masturbatory
insanity.[13] According to Henry Maudsley, who was the
foremost psychiatrist of his age, the prognosis for this
disease was hopeless. "The sooner he [the masturba-
tor] sinks to his degraded rest," he wrote in 1867,
"the better for the world which is well rid of him."[14]
Since Maudsley believed that the disease was incurable, he offered no remedy for it. Many other physicians,
however, thought that it was curable by means of sexual surgery.

The following excerpt is from a letter to a colleague
written by Luther V. Bell (1806–1862) on October 9,
1856. Bell was a prominent American psychiatrist and
one of the founders of the Association of Medical Su-
perintendents of American Institutions for the Insane
(now the American Psychiatric Association).

> I have often been consulted as to tying up the sper-
> matic arteries, the vasa deferentia, and the removal of
> the testes in forms of insanity connected with spermat-
> orrhoea. I have known it done repeatedly. In one case
> Dr. ——— castrated a clean-gone onanist [masturbator]
> who subsequently rallied, became an active man, and
> the doctor told me that he never met him that he did
> not receive his blessing for the great favor he had con-
> ferred upon him.[15]

Many similar cases were reported in the medical literature. The following account, from the *Boston Medical and Surgical Journal* in 1884, is typical:

Believing . . . that removing the testicles would remove the great source of difficulty [masturbation], I
recommended castration, with the confident expecta-
tion that it would prove successful. He was so misera-
ble, and life itself had become such a burden to him,
that he was not only willing to submit to the operation,
but urged me to perform it, which I did on the 29th of
November. . . . He has now the appearance of good
health, is cheerful and happy, can walk miles with as
much ease and elasticity as anyone, and with every
prospect of good health and a life of usefulness, he is
actively engaged in making arrangements to go into
business.[16]

The treatment of masturbation by means of surgery
reached its apogee, as might be expected, when the patient had "only" a clitoris. According to the conven-
tional medical wisdom of the late nineteenth century,
"it was irrelevant to a woman's feelings whether she
had sex organs or not."[17] While (male) doctors could
never quite convince themselves or the public that the
proper treatment for male masturbation was penec-
tomy, they did convince themselves and at least some
women that the proper treatment for female masturbation was clitoridectomy. The credit for this discovery
belongs to Isaac Baker Brown, a prominent London
surgeon who later became the president of the Medical
Society of London. He introduced the operation of
clitoridectomy around 1858, because he believed that
masturbation caused hysteria, epilepsy, and convul-
sive diseases.[18] One woman who had been castrated for
the "sexual perversion of masturbation" wrote back to
her castrator to report: "My condition is all I could

desire. I know and feel that I am well; I never think of
self-abuse; it is foreign and distasteful to me."[19]

Even as late as 1900, masturbation was still considered to justify the following surgical procedure:

> The prepuce is drawn well forward, the left forefinger
> inserted within it down to the root of the glans, and a
> nickelplated safety pin introduced from the outside
> through the skin and mucous membrane is passed hori-
> zontally for half an inch or so past the tip of the left
> finger and then brought out through the mucous mem-
> brane and skin so as to fasten from the outside. An-
> other pin is similarly fixed on the opposite side of the
> prepuce. With the foreskin looped up, any attempt at
> erection causes painful dragging on the pins, and mas-
> turbation is effectually prevented. In about a week
> some ulceration of the mucous membrane will allow
> greater movement and will cause less pain; then the
> pins can, if needful, be introduced in a new place, but
> the patient is already convinced that masturbation is
> not necessary to his existence, and a moral as well as a
> material victory has been gained.[20]

How docilely people then accepted such brutal medical interventions, and how docilely they still accept
similar barbarities. Then, the quacks claimed that masturbation was pathological—and proved it by torturing
the masturbator and calling it treatment. Now they insist that masturbation is healthful—and prove it by in-
venting the disease of masturbatory orgasmic inadequacy.[21]

Since masturbation was principally a male disease,
the fury of anti-masturbatory surgery was vented

mainly on men. For women there awaited sexual operations undreamt of in medically less advanced times.
The most important—because it was the most widely
practiced—of these procedures was the removal of both
normal ovaries, known eponymically as "Battey's operation," so named after Robert Battey, the American
surgeon who developed it in 1872.[22] During the next
three decades this procedure was performed on thousands of women, in the United States as well as in
Europe.

Then, as now, women brought a variety of complaints about their bodies, and especially about their
menstruation, to their physicians. Battey's operation—
which he called "normal ovariotomy," revealing a candor characteristic of a medical era when therapeutic
quackery had no reason yet to cloak itself behind
medical euphemisms—was introduced as a cure for the
diseases ostensibly responsible for these "female
complaints." Since the operation cured mythological
(nonexistent) diseases—such as pelvic neurosis, oopho-
romania, and ovarian epilepsy* [23]—it was considered to
be very successful and quickly became fashionable. In fact, physicians who hesitated to recommend
or perform the operation when it was believed to be indicated were condemned as "wanting in humanity"
and were even accused of criminal neglect of their patients. Because of the obscure nature of the diseases it
was supposed to cure, removal of both normal ovaries

---

* In the 1880s, these diagnoses were accepted (as the names of real
diseases) by the medical profession and the public—in the same way
that diagnoses such as anorgasmia and schizophrenia are accepted
today.

(causing a surgically induced menopause) was soon regarded as a veritable panacea—not a surprising consequence in view of Battey's own claims for it.

Battey was the first man in medical history to try to induce the menopause deliberately, surgically—as a cure. His reasoning was as follows: "I have hoped through the intervention of the great nervous revolution which ordinarily accompanies the climacteric, to uproot and remove serious sexual disorders and reestablish general health."[24] But Battey never restricted the indications for his operation to "sexual disorders" (whatever that term may have meant to him and his contemporaries). From the start, he advocated bilateral oophorectomy on young women—the average age of the patients operated on was about thirty—for "any grave disease which is either dangerous to life or destructive to health and happiness, which is incurable by other and less radical means."[25] That certainly left plenty of room for justifying the operation. In 1877, only five years after introducing the procedure, Battey reidentified the indications for it, adding specifically "cases of insanity or epilepsy caused by uterine or ovarian disease."[26] Later, he refined the indications for surgery—adding such fictional diseases as "oophoro-mania, oophoro-epilepsy, and oophoralgia."[27]

By the 1880s, Battey's operation was widely accepted as a treatment for ovarian neuralgia, severe dysmenorrhea (painful menstruation), epilepsy, nymphomania, and insanity. James Marion Sims (1813–1883), the father of American gynecological surgery, endorsed the procedure, for which the mortality rate ranged

from 20 to 33 percent. Moreover, testimonials from
grateful patients proved the effectiveness of the therapy and the correctness of the theory behind it. In
1896, a patient wrote to her doctor: "At times I became almost desperate enough to take my life and end
my sufferings. . . . I am now a well, happy, and cheerful girl, and do not feel like the same person at all."[28]

The claim that bilateral oophorectomy was a cure for
insanity might have been one of the reasons for the reaction that finally set in against the operation. At the
Pennsylvania State Hospital, in Norristown, a whole
ward was established for women undergoing the cure.
But hystero-epilepsy was one thing, institutionalized
insanity was quite another. "Gynecologists," observed
a critic of Battey's operation, "will never empty the lu-
natic asylums."[29] However, no one can say that they
didn't try, even if they had to "sacrifice"—to the greater
glory of God and the mythological diseases of a medical profession bent on empire-building—tens of thousands of normal ovaries.

Although doctors now seem eager to enable persons
to perform sexually, regardless of how or with whom—
until recently they were just as eager to disable persons
with "perverse" erotic interests from satisfying their
sexual appetites. Such sexually disabling operations—
for homosexuals† as well as for men who like to wear

† The belief that homosexuality is a disease was, until quite recently,
medical dogma. Many physicians, and especially psychiatrists, still
think so. Karl Menninger's views are typical. "We cannot, like Gide,"
he writes in 1963, "extol homosexuality. We do not, like some, con-
done it. We regard it as a symptom. . . ."[30] That in American psy-

feminine clothing (called transvestites)‡—were popular both before and after the Second World War (especially in Scandinavian countries). The following example is a classic.

> The patient was considered to have been homosexual from birth. . . . His homosexual activity is decidedly more pronounced during the active phases of his illness [paranoia]. . . . Castrated at the age of 46. . . . His psychic reaction to the operation was completely consistent with his paranoid attitude: the doctor has disabled him.[33]

The following report about the surgical treatment of a male transvestite illustrates the complex collusion between patient and doctor that often obtains in such cases.

> The [patient was] a medical student, later a doctor, who was transvestite. Up to his 5th year dressed as girl. Later preferred feminine attire, wore corsets, silk stockings and high heeled shoes. Masturbated daily from his 5th year, at a later stage 5–8 times daily. . . . Unable to concentrate on studies—only "slept or mas-

---

chiatry homosexuality continues to be considered a disease, and the conversion of the homosexual to heterosexual conduct a form of treatment, is evidenced by the chapter on this subject in the latest (1974) edition of the authoritative *American Handbook of Psychiatry*. In it, Charles Socarides, the leading psychoanalytic advocate of stigmatizing homosexuals as sick, describes the homosexual act as a "fix [that] may be likened to the effects of the opium alkaloids."[31] The unremitting hostility of psychiatrists and psychoanalysts to homosexuals is, in my opinion, now greatly underestimated, especially by homosexual organizations and their leaders.

‡ The future of this disease, too, seems bleak. Feminine underwear for men is now in brisk demand at one of the most famous London department stores: "In the men's department of Marks and Spencer there are stacks and stacks of women's knickers, described as polyester hipsters, in a bewildering variety of shades. . . ."[32]

turbated." Castration at own request when 23 years
old. Two days later spontaneous erection. Six days
later—day of release from hospital—coitus with orgasm
and ejaculation for the first time. Potent for 4 months
after castration, followed by impotency. . . . In the
hope of feminization, had an ovary implantation 11
months after castration. Took position as governess—
and requested surgeon to remove penis. The surgeon
. . . performed a plastic operation whereby penis was
hidden in the perineum. This occurred one year after
castration. Two months later the patient . . . had the
sexual impulses of a man. Intimate with a female student. Four months after the plastic operation had penis
replaced in its natural position. Erection every night.
Had coitus and maintained potency. . . . He passed
his final examinations and wrote five years later that
everything was fine—he had become a pathologist.[34]

During the last decade, the psychiatric scenario
about "sexual inversion" itself underwent an inversion.
In 1973, the American Psychiatric Association deleted
"homosexuality per se" from its official list of mental
diseases.[35] However, homosexuality remained a disease
if the person was dissatisfied with it.*

Although psychogenic impotence bears striking similarities to the devout Jew's lack of appetite for pork,
the former phenomenon is widely regarded as a disease, while the latter never is. Calling unwanted be-

* Although dissatisfaction with heterosexuality is not yet considered
to be a disease, the view that a person's displeasure with his or her
own sexual disposition constitutes a disease is now firmly established
in psychiatry and sexology. Dissatisfaction with one's own anatomical-
chromosomal sex, called transsexualism, is an example. It is discussed
on pages 86–92.

havior a disease is crucially important: it is the first step that leads to the acceptance of various interventions—from psychological therapies to penile prostheses —as bona fide treatments. The modern surgical cures of impotence stand in striking contrast to—indeed, are the mirror images of—some earlier treatments. Formerly, doctors sought to disable certain men who were sexually potent from being able to perform—typically, by castration; now they try to enable certain men who are sexually impotent to perform—typically, by means of implanting sexual prostheses. These devices are of two kinds—rigid and inflatable. The first technique consists of the implantation of one or two semirigid silicone rods into the spongy tissues of the penis. This produces a permanent erection which the patient must conceal with a jock strap or tight shorts—a strange cure, if ever there was one, but many doctors and patients seem to like it.

Frank Gerow, a Baylor University plastic surgeon, stresses that the issue of how the man became impotent is not important for the surgeon. "The surgeon," he says, "merely serves as a technician who implants the [penile] prosthesis so that the patient is able to use his penis for satisfying coital function. . . . What the impotent patient is saying when he comes to me is: 'Leave me alone with my psychoneurosis; cure my impotence.' The implant can do that."[36]

This is a curious claim, since the rigid penile implant creates a permanent erection—a sort of mechanical priapism. (Priapism is a persistent erection of the penis due to disease rather than to sexual desire.) The result is a veritable "dildoization" of the penis—the male gen-

ital organ being converted from a live, emotionally re-
sponsive bodily part into a dead mechanical device.

In addition to the rigid penile implant, with its obvious drawbacks, surgeons have also developed a so-
called inflatable penile prosthesis. This consists of two
expandable balloonlike cylinders which the surgeon in-
serts into the corpora cavernosa (the spongy tissue of
the penis that fills with blood in normal erection). The
cylinders are connected by tubing to a small reservoir
buried behind the abdominal wall, and to a pump in-
serted into the scrotum. To make the penis erect, the
man squeezes the pump, forcing fluid into the cylinders
and distending the penis. A release valve on the pump
reverses the process.

F. Brantley Scott, professor of urology at the Baylor
University College of Medicine and one of the de-
velopers of this device, recommends its use not only for
organic but also for psychogenic impotence. "I see no
valid objection," he says, "to surgical treatment of psychogenic erectile impotence. . . . I realized that the
process of erection in the human being is a hydraulic
phenomenon, and we developed the first hydraulic
prosthesis for the treatment of erectile impotence."[37]
Scott himself has already performed about 250 implan-
tations of his inflatable prosthesis. According to the
manufacturer, about 1,500 patients have received a hydraulic prosthesis.[38]

It is easy to see why doctors would like this sexual-
surgical gimmickry: besides feeding their therapeutic
megalomania, it feeds their pocketbooks. The inflatable
penis, installed, costs $9,000, while the silicone-rod
penis, installation again included, costs a mere $3,500.[39]

It is more difficult to see why patients would like such mechanized male members, but evidently they do. Doctors performing these operations claim that "implanted men are among the happiest of the patients they have ever seen."[40] Perhaps these men like to deceive themselves. Perhaps they like to deceive their wives or women in general. Sexual researchers have discovered that some men receiving penile prostheses do not tell their wives about the surgery—preferring to put their new-found sexual powers to use with other partners. We have long known that forbidden fruit tastes especially sweet. We must now add to this that perhaps fake fruit (especially in the area of human eroticism) does also. The suspicion that deception plays a significant role in the therapeutic effect of these operations receives further support from one of the most ardent advocates of the prosthetic penis. "It's important," says Frank Gerow, commenting on what the man's sexual partner ought to be told about the operation, "that women not be superfamiliar with what's being done. This is a man's operation for a man's problem."[41] He said it.

As if realizing the shortcomings of penile prostheses, surgeons have also developed a totally different type of operation for the treatment of impotence—one whose aim is to restore the organ to its natural function. Modeled after the coronary bypass surgery, this operation is called penile bypass surgery: as the former procedure is intended to increase the patient's blood supply to the heart, so the latter is intended to increase the blood supply to the penis. The treatment is based on the assumption that impotence may be due to insufficient

penile circulation—a condition some physicians believe
to be far more common than generally recognized.
"Vascular disease which is known to affect the heart,
the brain, and the kidneys is now being shown to be responsible for as many as 80% of cases of organic impotence," asserts Dr. Adrian Zorgniotti, clinical professor
of urology at New York University.[42]

Penile bypass surgery, the treatment that some urol-
ogists now recommend for impotence, is difficult and
dangerous—and the operative results are dubious. Still,
the existence and official acceptance of this and other
surgical techniques for the treatment of impotence
raise some practical questions: Will Blue Shield, com-
mercial health insurance carriers, and National Health
Insurance (should there be such a thing) pay for such
surgery? If so, at what age, if any, will there be a
cutoff?†

The disease most recently discovered by sexologists
is transsexualism—a condition tailor-made for our sur-
gical-technological age.[44] The diagnosis is based on the
individual's desire to change his or her chromosomally
defined sexual identity: in short, transsexualism is that
"condition" which justifies amputating the individual's normal sex organs and creating, by means
of reconstructive surgery, imitations of the sex organs
appropriate to the opposite of the person's real sex.
These operations are now accepted—in both medicine
and law—as bona fide medical treatments.[45]

The surgical technology of these operations—turning

† If a story in *Time* magazine is to be believed, "tens of thousands
of U.S. males ranging in age from under 19 to over 80" have already
received penile implants.[43]

men into fake women, and women into fake men[46]—is
enormously complex. A short excerpt from a description of the male-to-female operation (which is performed about four times more often than the reverse)
should suffice here:

> A perineal pocket for the neo-vaginal canal is then
> constructed by dissecting down into the perineum
> under the prostate and urethra and anterior to the rec-
> tum. The skin from the penis is inverted as one would
> turn a sock inside out and tucked down into the peri-
> neal pocket. . . . The urethra is shortened and im-
> planted in a more natural location just at the top of the
> vaginal opening. . . . We feel that this process creates
> realistic and functional external genitalia as well as a
> functioning vagina. In a minor third-stage operation in
> several patients, we were able to use redundant tissue
> to construct a neo-clitoris.[47]

How do the "transsexers"—the psychologists, psychiatrists, endocrinologists, and surgeons engaged in the
business of validating individuals as transsexuals and
transforming them into facsimiles of the opposite sex—
decide on whom to operate? Although some surgeons,
especially abroad, are reported to operate on all comers
who can afford their fees, "reputable" American doctors are inordinately proud of their selection procedures for identifying the proper candidates for these
operations. These procedures are of two kinds, each
very revealing. First, the male transsexual candidate
must be able to pass as a woman—that is, must be able
to prove that he can assume the socially stereotypical
feminine role. Second, the candidate must be able to
pass an enormous number of psychological and psychi-

atric tests—ostensibly to establish that he or she is not
psychotic and will benefit from the therapy. The former criterion is crassly sexist (anti-feminist).[48] The latter, as the following case history illustrates, is simply a
sham:

> The patient, a 30-year-old female-to-male transsexual
> . . . had been cosmetically altered to resemble a male
> in multi-staged procedures between 1970 to 1972. By
> April of 1972 the patient had received a mastectomy,
> radical hysterectomy, bilateral oophorectomy [removal
> of the ovaries], and phalloplasty [construction of a
> "penis"]. Before these procedures, the patient had
> been screened as a candidate for transsexual conver-
> sion by a team consisting of an endocrinologist, urol-
> ogist, gynecologist, psychologist, psychiatrist, and so-
> cial worker, and had been given an extensive medical
> workup. . . . [A résumé of the patient's history fol-
> lows.]
>
> After [transsexual] surgery, the patient began to
> reintegrate into the community as a man. He started
> college, worked part-time and began to date heterosex-
> ual women who knew nothing of his past. Each of
> these relationships ended because he was unable to
> achieve penetration with his surgically constructed
> phallus and also because he disclosed the fact that he
> had been a woman. The patient's inability to have suc-
> cessful relationships with women created increasing
> feelings of helplessness and depression. These feelings
> were present despite the fact that he had presumably
> understood before surgery that he would be unable to
> achieve erection and penetration. [In 1976, the patient
> made a third unsuccessful suicide attempt.] . . . The
> surgical conversion from female to male was done in an

attempt to alleviate the risk of suicide, which was considered to be closely linked to the patient's gender dys-
phoria.[49]

Psychiatrists have long been in the habit of responding to individuals who threaten to kill themselves by
punishing or rewarding them: thus, they have coer-
cively hospitalized, electroshocked, and drugged such
patients—or granted them therapeutic abortions
(which were denied to individuals who asked for them
directly and nonthreateningly). Since the discovery of
transsexualism, psychiatrists have expanded the uses of
the "risk [i.e., threat] of suicide"—making it one of
their criteria for granting transsexing as a life-saving
procedure.

People now want to know whether sex-change surgery helps the transsexual. Does it work? Such questions, though seemingly reasonable, are misleading. We
might just as well ask whether castration helped the
masturbator. Did it work? The trouble with psychiatric
treatments, as I noted some years ago, is that all of
them work, and none of them work.[50] However, therapists tend to be doers rather than thinkers: they prefer
to make claims and counterclaims about whether certain treatments work rather than reflect about what
they and their patients are doing with and to one another. Thus, instead of scrutinizing the nature of
"transsexualism," sexologists are now busily attacking
and defending sex-change operations.

The controversy about transsexual surgery broke into
the open when, in August 1979, the Johns Hopkins
Hospital, a pioneer in sex-change operations, an-

nounced that it "stopped the surgery after research failed to show any objective improvement in the patients' lives."[51] The research to which this announcement alluded, and which was published at the same time, was a study by Jon K. Meyer, the psychiatrist-director of the Johns Hopkins sexual consultation program. Having reviewed the outcome of transsexual surgery at Hopkins, Meyer concluded that the surgery "does not cure what is essentially a psychiatric disturbance."[52] To arrive at that conclusion, there was, however, no need to do any research. The assertion that surgery does not cure a psychiatric disturbance is what philosophers call an analytical truth—that is, a truth inherent in the meaning of the terms of reference. Asserting that a sterile woman cannot become pregnant is a typical example. Having first deceived the public by promoting transsexual surgery as therapy, sexologists now continue to deceive it by opposing such surgery as insufficiently therapeutic. But transsexualism is not a disease; surgical operations creating fake males and fake females are not treatments; and some transsexed individuals are satisfied with their decision to undergo the operations while some others are not.

The defenders of sex-change operations have, of course, no difficulty in answering critics like Meyer who accept transsexualism as a bona fide disease and object to the surgery only because it is not sufficiently therapeutic. Indeed, their defense is double-pronged, technical as well as theoretical. The technicians assert that their operative procedures are now much better than they used to be, making studies based on old operations scientifically worthless. The theoreticians assert, or rather reassert, their favorite justification for sex surgery (or any other intervention)—namely, that it "saves lives."

The technical justification of sex-change operations is exemplified by the following remarks of David Forester, president of the Oklahoma Gender Identity Foundation and a pioneer of modern transsexual surgical techniques: "Many of the cases of this study [Meyer's] are early ones, when procedures were crude. If a male-to-female transsexual is given a small vagina in which she can't have intercourse and external genitalia that look like meat in a butcher shop, naturally that is going to affect adjustment."[53] As an X-ray allows a surgeon to look behind the patient's skin into his body, so the language of the transsexing surgeon allows us to look behind his "technique" to his soul—and gain information that we ignore at our own peril.

The argument that a particular intervention is therapeutic because it saves lives—by preventing patients from committing suicide—is a favorite rhetorical device of the modern psychiatrist. Harry Benjamin—who invented the disease and is therefore the acknowledged "father of transsexualism"—puts the argument (in reply to Meyer's criticism) as follows: "What both treatments [insulin for diabetes, sex-reassignment for transsexuals] accomplish is the preservation of the life of the patient. Otherwise, many of these people would commit suicide. There is no doubt, in my mind, that sex-reassignment surgery can be life-saving and frequently is just that."[54] But the analogy between the diabetic and the transsexual is specious, to say the least. If insulin is withheld from the diabetic, he dies from his disease, not from suicide. Unlike the diabetic, the transsexual cannot die of his disease. Out of despair, the "transsexual," like anyone else, may kill himself; or, like anyone else, he may threaten suicide to extort something he wants from family, friends, or physicians. Nevertheless, Benjamin contends that, for the transsexual, "sex-reassignment surgery can be life-saving," and must be regarded as a bona fide treatment.‡

The idea that human beings—especially women—are improperly made sexual machines whose performance can, and should, be put aright by surgeons continues to fascinate the medical imagination. Concerning the question of how the female sexual anatomy ought to be fixed up, we run into the same reversal of the judgments of a century ago that we met in connection with masturbation. Then, the normal woman was an asexual being; that notion justified the belief that the sexually sensitive clitoris was an abnormality and that clitoridectomy was a therapy. Now the normal woman is an infinitely sexual being; that notion justifies the belief

‡ By resorting to such reasoning (if it can be called that), virtually anything displeasing to a person could be defined as a disease and its ostensibly medical alteration accepted as a treatment. Perhaps Oedipus Rex was not really a tragic hero, but a sick patient: he was suffering from "transvisualism" and sought to cure himself by putting out his own eyes. Some people (called psychotic) feel tortured by having eyes that "see too much" and seek to blind themselves. Were such a person to threaten suicide unless his doctor removed his eyes, would that make blinding him a life-saving procedure and establish transvisualism as a bona fide disease? Or, to take a less extreme example, let us suppose that an elderly person threatened to kill himself unless a plastic surgeon made him look more youthful. Would that make his "condition" a disease ("trans-chronologicalism" might be a good name for it), and cosmetic surgery making old people look younger a life-saving procedure?

that the sexually sensitive clitoris ought to be made
more use of than nature has provided for it and that
surgical interventions "making the clitoris more acces-
sible" to the penis are forms of therapy:

> [A]n Ohio gynecologist is proposing that millions of
> American women are ideal surgical candidates for a
> vaginal reconstruction he has devised to awaken and
> enrich their sex lives. Dr. James C. Burt, 56, of Dayton,
> exhibits his stunning 31-year-old blonde wife, Joan, as
> demonstrable proof of his claim that reconstructing the
> vagina to make the clitoris more accessible to direct
> penile stimulation enables a woman to have more fre-
> quent and more intense orgasms. Once only "randomly
> vaginally orgasmic," Mrs. Burt describes the operation
> as a "complete success." Over the past 12 years, Dr.
> Burt has performed the operation in all stages of its ev-
> olution . . . on some 4,000 women. . . . He calls the
> ideal candidate for his operation a heterosexual
> woman who climaxes readily with clitoral manipu-
> lation but who is rarely if ever orgasmic during coitus
> —and even then not intensely—and who wants coital
> orgasm.[55]

In the meantime, in the less "developed" parts of the
world, the male attack on the female genital continues
by more traditional means. The following mutilations,
still popular in Third World countries, make a mockery
of American politicians' smug declarations about human rights:

> Clitoridectomy is practised in the Yemen, Saudi Ara-
> bia, Ethiopia, Sudan, Egypt, Iraq, Jordan, Syria, the
> Ivory Coast, among the Dogons of the Niger, the Man-
> dingos of Mali, the Toucouleu in the north of Senegal,

and the Peuls, and among many other African tribes. . . . In some other countries . . . it is also necessary to sew the women up. . . . After having cut, without the benefit of anesthetic, part of the large lips, they are brought together by piercing them with pins. This way they grow together, except for a space for the passage of blood and urine. The young wife must, before her wedding night, have it reopened with a razor. Her husband can, moreover, always insist on having his wife sewn up again if he is thinking of leaving her for some time.[56]

Set in the context of contemporary Western sexual-surgical (and other medical) practices, such mutilations show us, in the starkest terms, how intensely modern men and women continue to fear embracing, decisively and responsibly, the proposition that human rights begin with the right to self-ownership.

What position should the state take toward sexual surgery? Are there some medical procedures that the state should permit, and others that it should prohibit? If so, on what moral, political, or scientific criteria should such decisions be based? These are difficult questions that go to the heart of the problems of modern political philosophy.

In general, our position on such questions will depend on whether we favor an authoritarian/paternalistic type of society or a libertarian/individualistic one. The authoritarian/paternalistic stance minimizes the problems generated by the foregoing questions, since it allows us to justify permitting some procedures and prohibiting others on the ground that doing so protects the integrity and well-being of the group and its dominant ethic. The libertarian/individualistic stance allows us no such escape. What it does enable us to do is to deal with the question by asserting that unless the sexual-surgical intervention in question entails the use of force or fraud, it is of no concern to the law. And if it does entail the use of force or fraud, then it is that aspect of the relationship and not the nature of the surgery that justifies, and indeed requires, the protection of the individual by the law.

As one man's meat is another man's poison, so one man's mutilation is another man's decoration, religious worship, or medical treatment. I consider, and no doubt many readers consider, ritual or routine circumcision, clitoridectomy, transsexual operations, and many of the other procedures described in this chapter as mutilations. Others, obviously, do not agree with this judgment. Why should our opinion be imposed on them or theirs on us?

The history of medicine is replete with mutilations that had been accepted, or are now accepted, as treatments: blood-letting, routine obstetrical episiotomies, prefrontal lobotomy, and jejuno-ileal bypass (for obesity) are just a few examples. In the final analysis, what constitutes medical treatment is a definition made by individuals or institutions. Regardless of who they are—patients, their families, physicians, the medical profession, the state—each will have his or her own reasons for categorizing some things as treatments and others as not treatments. Since among the reasons for such a classification, so-called facts, rationality, or science will play a very subordinate role, it seems best to

recognize this fact, accept the quasi-theological character of medicine as a social enterprise, and erect a wall
between medicine and the state maximally impervious
to the rhetorical incantations and financial temptations
of each directed toward the other.[57]

Sex Education

6

RELIGION
AS SEX EDUCATION

Like many of our most cherished clichés, the term "sex education" is hopelessly imprecise and needlessly provocative. Is sex education (especially for children) instruction in anatomy, genetics, and reproduction or indoctrination in certain opinions about erotic practices, teenage pregnancy, and the population explosion? Is it biology or ideology? Science or religion?

Clearly, only the purely biological aspects of sexuality are a matter of science. And biology has always been, and should be, taught in schools. But it is an insignificant element in sex education, which is concerned with human sexual behavior.

Since human behavior denotes the actions of moral agents, all behavior is, in part at least, a matter of eth-

ics. Sexual behavior is very much a matter of ethics.
Hence, since time immemorial, persons who proposed
to teach people about sex had but two choices: to embrace and endorse the accepted, traditional sexual
ways of the group, or to explore and enjoin sexual principles and practices at odds with those ways. There is
no such thing as value-free sex education, nor can there
be.

Many people now believe that sex education, like an-
tibiotics or television, is an invention of the modern
scientific mind. That is a naive belief. Sex education is
as old as mankind. All religions are intensely concerned
with the regulation of sexual conduct. In order to place
modern sex education in its proper historical context,
let us look at the principal sexual teachings of ancient
Judaism and early Christianity.*

The Jewish attitude toward sexuality is inseparable
from the Jewish attitude toward marriage and procreation. In Judaism, marriage is not a personal choice; it is
a religious duty. For example, a fifth-century Talmudic
authority states: "If a [widower] has children he may
desist from procreation, but not from further marriage."[1] However, procreation is even more sacred than
marriage. If, for example, after ten years of marriage a
wife has produced no children, Jewish law enjoined the
husband to divorce her and marry another woman or to
take a second wife.[2] (Polygamy was never widely prac-

* Since in the hands of many contemporary commentators both
Jewish and Christian sexual teachings have become so modernized as
to bear no similarity to the original doctrines of these creeds, in this
chapter I shall confine myself to the old, or "orthodox," forms of these
religions.

ticed by the Jews.) Jewish authorities differ on how many children a man is expected to father—the responsibility being solely the man's. While some rabbis believed that it was permissible to practice birth control after one male and one female child had been produced, this was by no means generally agreed upon. For example, Moses Maimonides (1135–1204) taught that "Although a man has fulfilled the mitzvah [religious duty], he is commanded by the Rabbis not to desist from procreation while he yet has the strength."[3]

The extent to which ancient Jewish sexual attitudes were influenced by the desire for offspring is illustrated by the biblical story of Lot. When the men of Sodom were besieging Lot's house demanding to be given two travelers (who were actually angels) for homosexual intercourse, Lot offered them instead his daughters, and was rewarded by being saved, with his daughters, from the destruction of the city.[4] Immediately after this, Lot's wife having been killed, the daughters make Lot drunk and commit incest with him in order to preserve his seed.[5]

Since marriage was a duty (and since the Jewish concept of society was patriarchal), bachelorhood was considered a crime. Because in the biblical story of creation man and woman together are called "man," rabbinic authorities went so far as to declare that "whoever is not married is not a man."[6] In the Middle Ages, in communities under Jewish self-government, the rabbinic courts employed all the powers vested in them—such as corporal punishment, fines, and excommunication—to compel bachelors to get married.[7]

Furthermore, since matrimony was a religious institution, marriage to an alien woman meant betraying the Jewish God. After exhorting the Israelites to show no mercy toward the Hittites and other neighboring tribes, Yahveh commands them: "Neither shalt thou make marriage with them. . . . For they will turn away thy son from following me, that they may serve other gods: so will the anger of the Lord be kindled against you, and destroy thee suddenly."[8]

The ancient Jews were a xenophobic, tribal people whose laws were directed toward maintaining the purity of their group identity. Perhaps precisely because the Jewish sex ethic was so intensely tribal and procreative, it was not anti-erotic. It was anti-Gentile. Thus, circumcision was regarded not merely as the bodily seal upon the covenant between the Jews and Yahveh, but also as a protection against going to hell. According to the Talmud, *Gehinnom* (the Hebrew name for hell) is reserved for Gentiles—and for Jewish men who have sexual relations with Gentile women: "Abraham our father comes and takes them [the circumcised Jews from *Gehinnom*] and receives them, with the exception of an Israelite who had intercourse with a Gentile woman. . . ."†[9]

In the Jewish sexual ethic, then, what is forbidden is

---

† Some exceptionally wicked Jews were also banished to *Gehinnom* —but only after their circumcision had been undone: "Israelites who are circumcised will not descend to *Gehinnom*. So that the heretics and the sinners in Israel shall not say, 'Inasmuch as we are circumcised we will not go to *Gehinnom*,' what does the Holy One, blessed be He, do? He sends an angel who extends the foreskin and they descend to *Gehinnom*."[10]

not erotic pleasure, but illicit erotic acts. In his excellent book, *Birth Control in Jewish Law*, David Feldman cites many Talmudic authorities in support of this "pro-sexual" character of Judaism.‡ One of these authorities (Rabbi Jacob ben Asher) contrasts prohibited adultery with the sexual freedom available in marriage: "But a man's own wife is permitted to him, and with her, he is allowed to do as he pleases. He may cohabit with her whenever he pleases, kiss her wherever he pleases, and cohabit naturally or unnaturally."[12]

Although in the ancient Jewish view of the world the woman occupies a decidedly secondary position, her conjugal right to sexual congress and her husband's duty to fulfill it are explicitly recognized in the Torah. This so-called conjugal debt falls due at specified times and varies according to the husband's ability and occupation. For example, if a man wants to engage in a type of work that would take him away from home for extended periods, he can do so only with his wife's permission.[13] Feldman emphasizes that in this view of marital relations, the sexual act becomes "the duty of the husband and the privilege of the wife. This is in contradistinction, for better or worse, to the Christian egalitarian view, and, for better, stands in neat contrast to the attitude deplored by modern writers, according

‡ The famed Jewish philosopher-sage Moses Maimonides explicitly rejected asceticism as sinful: "One might say: inasmuch as jealousy, passion, love of honor . . . may bring about a man's downfall, I will therefore remove myself to the other extreme. I will refrain from meat and wine or marriage or a pleasant home or attractive garments. . . . This is an evil way and forbidden. He who follows these practices is a sinner."[11]

to which sex is seen as the man's right and the woman's duty."* [14]

The sex educational character of these rules and regulations could not be more explicit. Indeed, the approval of erotic enjoyment in the Jewish sex ethic culminates in the articulation, as religious teaching, of what we now call sexual technique. "Just as a lion tramples and devours and has no shame, so a boorish man strikes and copulates and has no shame," is the image the Jewish sages use to condemn men who are "premature ejaculators"; and they urge them to adopt this supposedly modern method: "Rather win her over with words of graciousness and seductiveness. Hurry not to arouse her passion until her mood is ready; begin in love; let her 'semination' (orgasm?) take place first."[16]

Although Jewish law recognizes the legitimacy of pleasure in the sex act, the act must be marital congress between a Jewish man and a Jewish woman. Non-Jews were proscribed as marital partners not only because they did not worship Yahveh but also because they were regarded as sexually perverted. Jewish scholars arrived at this idea by means of the following reasoning. The serpent had infected Eve, and through her all of mankind, with "lasciviousness." Through their wanderings in the Sinai, the people of Israel were cleansed of this sin, but "the heathen who were not at Sinai

---

* In December 1979, a rabbinical court in Israel ordered a thirty-two-year-old man, who was a model husband but refused to have intercourse with his wife, "to perform his conjugal duties or pay 36 grains of silver a week until he does so." Rabbinical courts have sole jurisdiction over marriages and divorces in Israel.[15]

remained addicted to those passions."† [17] Jewish law
even decreed the death penalty for animals that men
used for sexual congress. Although such an animal has
"not sinned . . . the law is justified in executing the
beast because it served as a tool for the downfall of a
human being."[19]

Consistent with this intensely interpersonal (rather
than individualistic) view of the sex act, Jewish law
strictly forbids masturbation. The practice is condemned unequivocally both in the Talmud and in ex-
tra-Talmudic literature. The Zohar calls masturbation
"a sin more serious than all the sins of the Torah."[20]
Jewish exegetes interpret the act as "murder" and say
that the guilty person "deserves death." Although this
was rhetorical hyperbole rather than an actual demand
for execution, it is nevertheless indicative of the Jewish
condemnation of sexual self-gratification. This prohibition rests, of course, on the view that the masturbator
destroys his "generative seed" and thus commits an act
not unlike murder.‡

Jewish law went further still. It regarded even invol-
untary (nocturnal) emissions as "partly sinful," because it did "not consider the man a helpless, innocent
victim in every case."[22] Taking into account the obvious connection between sexual stimulation during the
day and subsequent seminal emission at night, the Jew-

† Medieval Christianity responded in kind, "decreeing that copulation with a Jew constituted a form of 'bestiality' and incurred the
same penances."[18]
‡ The fact that in biblical and rabbinic Hebrew "offspring" is often
called "seed" may have facilitated this imagery. Like other people of
antiquity, the ancient Hebrews believed that women also possessed and
emitted "seed."[21]

ish law commanded men to avoid such stimulation—a
prohibition that went so far as to forbid touching one's
penis: "The law definitely prohibits touching one's
genitals—the unmarried man never, and the married
man only in connection with urination."[23] This is why,
among orthodox Jews, one of the most important aspects of bladder training is to admonish the boy not to
finger his penis: "'Without hands!' is the admonitory
cry of a parent seeing his or her son attempting to pass
water with digital aid. Better a bad aim than a bad
habit!"[24]

Psychologically, the Jewish religious prohibition
against touching one's penis symbolizes that the male
sexual organ belongs to the Jewish God. Theologically,
the Jewish religious prescription of circumcision symbolizes the covenant between Yahveh and Abraham
(and all Jews). These two sets of practices are clearly
connected: only the circumcised male can urinate
without touching his penis—the uncircumcised male
having to pull back the foreskin. Jewish ritual circumcision is a necessary complement to the Jewish religious prohibition against touching one's penis.

The Christian moral premise—that chastity is the supreme sexual-ethical virtue, and that all sexual pleasure
is wicked—entailed a significant downgrading of marriage from the position it occupied in Judaism. Although marriage later became a Christian sacrament,
the early Christians ranked matrimony far below celibacy, as Roman Catholics still do (hence the required
celibacy of their priests and nuns). The most novel feature of Christianity lay, indeed, in identifying chastity

—that is, abstinence from sexual acts and pleasure of all kinds—as a virtue, and in elevating it above all other virtues. In fact, the Greeks, like all primitive (non-Christian) people, had no special word for chastity. When the Church Fathers, who wrote in Greek, spoke of the new Christian virtue, they employed the term *agneia*—which means a "rite of aversion or mourning"—and extended it to cover this new idea.[25]

The religious requirement of chastity set a moral standard to which few, if any, human beings could adhere; and that failure in turn served admirably to confirm the image of mankind as innately wicked.[26] Since sex was considered sinful, how did the early Christians accept and then even sanctify marriage? By an ingenious chain of rationalizations: they maintained that the pleasurable satisfaction of lust was a grave sin, even in marriage, but argued that marriage was a permissible arrangement because it was "a remedy against sin" that led to producing more virgins to worship Jesus.[27] Thus, they remained hostile to matrimony, viewing it in terms that resemble the language of contemporary critics of this institution. In his classic study, *Sexual Relations in Christian Thought,* Derrick Bailey documents how the Church Fathers "continued to regard matrimony as a concession to the inordinate desires of fallen humanity," calling marriage a "sad tragedy" and a "galling burden," "servitude" and "an oppressive bondage."[28]

Because chastity was "pure" and coitus "impure," the ministerial office could not be "defiled" by coitus.[29] Because sexual activity was "a complete evil," the absence of sexual activity came to be thought a complete

good: "Virginity worked miracles."[30] The medieval
Scholastics thus arrived at a valuation of coitus that did
justice to their fame for making moral ambiguity an intellectual achievement. Coital pleasure, they declared,
was "not sinful as such, but it could not be pursued for
its own sake without sin: within marriage the sin was
always venial; outside of marriage, it was mortal."[31]

Although Luther accepted marriage, he continued to
teach that the sex act is "always unclean" (he was, after
all, not a Lutheran, but a Catholic priest). Luther's
view on sex illustrates, moreover, that the medical attitude toward it is neither new nor scientific. Maintaining
that "I will not concede to nature that it [marriage] is
no sin," Luther called matrimony "a medicine, a hospital for the sick."[32] This revealing medical metaphor pervades early Lutheranism and becomes a powerful
influence on seventeenth-century Anglicanism. John
Donne, for example, spoke of men using their wives "in
medicinam"—which he considered "the lowest of all
employments of matrimony," whose main purpose, in
his view, was the avoidance of fornication.[33] Thus, the
idea that the function of woman is to be "used as remedy for sin," deeply embedded in Christian theology,[34]
led to the creation of a Christian sex education inconsistent with the Church's teaching about the spiritual
equality of the sexes.

The ancient Jews believed that it was their religious
duty to enjoy life in all its varied dimensions, including
the sexual. Still, the Jewish sexual ethic was no more
permissive than the Christian. In Judaism, sexual relations were either prescribed (that is, in marriage, at

RELIGION AS SEX EDUCATION

certain times) or prohibited (that is, outside of marriage, at certain other times).

By contrasting the beliefs and practices of the early (Jewish) Christians with those of the (non-Christian) Jews we can better appreciate the origin and nature of Christianity as an ascetic Jewish sect. There existed several such sects around the time Christianity arose, the Essenes being one of the best known. Some authorities believe that Jesus might have been one of their adherents. The Dead Sea Scrolls, discovered in 1947, provide strong evidence that the early Christian doctrines about celibacy, divorce, and monogamy were drawn directly from ascetic Jewish dissidents—probably Essenes—and not from Greco-Roman sources as previously thought.[35] The Scrolls stipulate, for example, that Jews who have experienced sexual intercourse or nocturnal emissions must purify themselves for three days before entering the "Temple city." They also forbid defecation on the Sabbath. Another ascetic Jewish sect, described by the philosopher Philo, flourished during the first century A.D. Its members—called the Therapeutae, a Greek word whose original meaning was "attendant" or "servant"—were said to be "unusually severe in their discipline and mode of life."[36]

To understand the early Christian attitude toward sex—in particular, valuing chastity and celibacy more highly than procreation and matrimony—these sexual precepts must be situated in their precise historical context. Accordingly, I propose to view Christian "chastitism" as a reaction against Jewish "matrimonialism." Jewish marriage was compulsory. According to Jewish law, there could (for all practical purposes) be no such thing as an unmarried Jewish male.[37] By making matrimony and procreation compulsory, the Jews thus spoiled eroticism—at least for those persons who valued liberty more highly than conformity.

The importance of the fact that the ancient Jews compelled their people to marry and procreate has been greatly underestimated in the history of theology and sexual ethics. Indeed, few things reveal as clearly or dramatically the Jewish origin of Christianity as does the fact that in the Christian imagery of society all *persons*—men and women—*are* (or must be) *married*. In other words, while the early Christians recognized *unmarried males* and *females*, they did not recognize (perhaps could not even imagine) *unmarried persons*. If this sounds strange at first, it is because the early Christians achieved a major social transformation by metaphorizing marriage and then literalizing the metaphor.[38]

For the Jews, marriage was an actual social relationship. It was the compulsory character of this relationship that the Jewish-Christian heretics sought to abolish. However, although their aim was to liberate men and women from the stranglehold of compulsory matrimony, they themselves could not conceive of unmarried persons as solitary individuals (a notion much more recent in human history than is generally realized). They solved their dilemma the same way many social problems have been and continue to be solved—namely, by a radical transformation of the meaning of certain key words and the creation of certain new social arrangements or institutions.

One of the key terms whose meaning the early Chris-

tians changed was marriage—extending it, at first probably metaphorically, to the relationship between the
unmarried person and the new deity, Jesus. Among
both Christian Jews and Jewish Jews, every adult was
still a married person, but with this difference: among
the latter, Jewish men had to be married to Jewish
women; whereas among the former, individuals (regardless of sex, race, or religious origin) could be married *literally*, to a member of the opposite sex—or
metaphorically, to Jesus (and later to the Church). By
the third century, this metaphor had the power of literal truth, as illustrated by the following argument by
St. Cyprian about the impossibility of marriage for a
Christian virgin: "If a husband come and see his wife
lying with another man, is he not indignant and mad-
dened? How indignant and angered then must Christ
our Lord and Judge be, when He see a virgin, dedicated to Himself, and consecrated to His holiness, lying
with a man! . . . She who has been guilty of this crime
is an adulteress, not against a husband, but Christ."[39]
Then, the metaphor of marriage to Christ was made literal to support the rhetoric of religion; now, the metaphor of sexual desire as disease is made literal to support the rhetoric of therapy.

The Jewish compulsion to marry is analogous to the
modern compulsion to drink or use certain drugs: in
each case, a person engages in a particular act; and in
each case, he often feels driven in the opposite direc-
tion, finding ecstasy in avoiding the act he had previously needed to perform.[40] Thus, the Christian teaching against marriage and for chastity (that is, for
marriage to Jesus) could be regarded as an act of liber-

ation from compulsory Jewish matrimony. If that is so, it would be a mistake to interpret the anti-matrimonialism of the early Christians as merely anti-sexual. Rather, the shift in emphasis was religious: the Jews worshipped Yahveh by compulsory matrimony; the Christians worshipped Jesus by voluntary chastity. Judaism thus promoted compulsory copulation in compulsory matrimony, whereas Christianity promoted voluntary chastity in voluntary celibacy.

It is misleading to contrast Jewish sensuality with Christian asceticism. In fact, both Jewish and Christian sexual codes aim at and prescribe pleasurable behaviors. The faithful Jew finds pleasure in marital coitus and procreation; the faithful Christian, in celibate chastity. The scientific mind rebels against this phenomenon and seeks to distort or destroy it. To such a mind, either the seeker or the avoider must be right and the other wrong. But that is not science; it is denial. In reality, social behavior is characterized by boundless diversity: what pleases some pains others.* Modern therapists often fail to grasp this simple fact. That failure, in turn, reveals their persistent inability to transcend their cultural biases—in particular their persistent longing to be "high" on sex and their projection of that longing onto both the "nature of man" and the "nature of human sexuality."

What about the sex education inherent in Islam, the creed fashioned largely out of Judaism and Christianity?[41] The Mohammedan sexual ethic resembles the

* I use the term "pleasure" here operationally, to denote the mental state of a person who attains his longed-for aim, whatever that aim might be. Some people get pleasure from eating, others from dieting.

Jewish sexual ethic, the most interesting difference between the two being that the former promises the
faithful boundless sexual enjoyment in heaven. For
"those that fear the majesty of their Lord," declares the
Koran, "there are two gardens. . . . [The faithful]
shall recline on couches lined with thick brocade, and
. . . shall dwell with bashful virgins . . . as fair as coral
and rubies. . . ."[42] Surely, this Islamic image of
heaven contradicts the widely held view that all religions are anti-sexual. Like the Old Testament, the
Koran is anti-feminine, but it is not anti-sexual.

The Mohammedan attitude toward women is an ex-
tension of the traditional Jewish attitude toward them
and a rejection of the Christian attempt to soften the
political distinctions between the sexes. Through his
prophet, Mohammed, Allah lays down these rules for
women: "Enjoin believing women to turn their eyes
away from temptations and to preserve their chastity;
to cover their adornments (except such as are nor-
mally displayed); to draw their veils over their
bosoms. . . ."[43]

In short, Judaism, Christianity, and Islam each frame
and prescribe a type of sex education. The sexual
teachings of these religions are partly similar, partly
different. The differences among them are epitomized
by the following features: In Judaism, marriage is compulsory, in Christianity chastity is valued more highly
than matrimony, and in Islam marriage is contingent
on property.† Both the Jewish and Christian heavens
are sexless, being in the presence of God constituting

† The Koran states: "Let those who cannot afford to marry live in
continence until Allah enriches them."[44]

the resurrected soul's principal pleasure. (The pious Jew is also promised a "wonderful banquet" in *Gan Eden*, the Jewish heaven.[45]) Only in Islam is there a promise, for the faithful (male), of heavenly sex after death.

7

SEX EDUCATION—
FOR CHILDREN

In the late 1960s, sex education programs were given in about half of America's public and parochial schools. Between 1966 and 1969, the federal government provided more than $2 million in grants to help states establish sex education projects. By 1978, the federal government's direct contribution to teenage sex education and birth control programs was approaching $150 million, with uncounted millions being funneled into such programs indirectly through the Department of Health, Education and Welfare.* [1]

* American sex education received one of its biggest boosts in 1966 when the U. S. Department of Health, Education and Welfare (HEW) placed the government's imprimatur on sex education and provided considerable aid for its adoption in the nation's schools. At the beginning of the 1966–67 school year, the U. S. Office of Education also gave sex education its official blessing.[2]

What do these programs encompass? What are the students taught? According to *Newsweek,* fourth and fifth graders see films showing "the male and female anatomy in detail and discuss the mechanism of erection and ejaculation and the role of the clitoris in sexual pleasure."[3] In Schenectady, New York, sixth graders are "taught the mechanics of sexual intercourse in 'medically and socially acceptable' vocabulary"[4] and high school students see "films . . . from which [they] are told they can receive the answers to such questions as: Is it harmful to the baby if a woman has intercourse with more than one man? Is sexual intercourse really a sin?"[5] In the same year, the chief administrator of the Watkins Glen, New York, school system acknowledged that since sex education was a regular part of the curriculum, he had been presenting such sex educational materials without seeking parental consent.[6]

Various reports about the actual operation of sex education programs in the public schools make it abundantly clear that in these courses children are taught a minimum of biological science and a maximum of an anti-interpersonal sexual ideology. For example, a curriculum guide for the seventh and eighth grades in the Humboldt County, California, schools in the late 1970s specified that "the student will develop an understanding of masturbation," will view films on masturbation, and will "learn the four philosophies of masturbation—traditional, religious, neutral, radical—by participating in a class debate."[7]

Professional sex educators promote masturbation because their model of human sexuality is mechanical.

The sexual organs are like so many levers which the child should learn to manipulate to obtain pleasure—and to tranquilize himself. "If the [sexual] feeling and tension bother you," advises a Planned Parenthood pamphlet, "you can masturbate. Masturbation cannot hurt you and it will make you more relaxed."[8] Probably not, if you are told to do it by the school authorities.

Education for Sexuality, by John Burt and Linda Meeks—a standard text for teachers of sex—exemplifies the same thrust toward the masturbatory model of sex. They offer a curriculum that begins with a mixed-group "bathroom tour" in the first grade. In the fourth grade, children receive detailed instruction about male and female genital anatomy and human intercourse. By the time the students reach the seventh grade, they will have been taught about the vagina and labia, the penis and clitoris, erection, ejaculation and orgasm, and the meaning of such words as "fellatio" and "cunnilingus."[9]

In addition to promoting, as a matter of sexual ideology, a masturbatory model of sex, sex education programs also have a very practical aim—namely, fertility control, especially among minorities. Planned Parenthood and the Sex Information and Education Council of the United States (SIECUS) have long held that this was one of the sex educators' main responsibilities. In 1966, an HEW pamphlet on family planning endorsed sex education projects as a means of "effective fertility control."†[10] The fact that the consequence of

† The business of systematically concealing a secular sexual ethic as medical science and teaching it in the public schools as sex education began between the two world wars. Ironically, a 1939 Public Health Service manual admonished that "Masturbation . . . is de-

sex education is an increased rate of illegitimate pregnancy (just as the consequence of drug education is an increased rate of drug abuse) has not weakened the credibility or legitimacy of these programs. On the contrary, the sex education lobby uses such statistics as evidence for a need for still more sex education—and the public falls for it. In 1976, 25 percent of all sexually active girls became pregnant by the time they were seventeen, and 33 percent became pregnant by the time they reached nineteen.[12] "The studies document that sex among teen-agers has escalated," says Alfred F. Moran, executive vice-president of Planned Parenthood of New York City. "But contraceptive use hasn't. Teenagers aren't getting the message that if they have sex, they shouldn't go without protection."[13]

Protection for whom? The promoters of sex education trying to reduce teenage pregnancy are not really interested in protecting teenagers from getting pregnant; they are interested in protecting society from teenage pregnancy! For that hypocrisy, too, our society is paying dearly. By 1977, one out of ten American female teenagers was pregnant—and most of them (87 percent of the blacks and 62 percent of the whites) went on to give birth.[14]

Since sex educators in the schools address themselves to the sexual behavior of human beings, it is inevitable that they should touch on some of the most intensely

structive because it breaks down self-confidence and self-control."[11] That, of course, was forty years ago. Then the U. S. Public Health Service didn't know any better. Today the Department of HEW knows all the scientific facts about sex, and only such facts are now taught in American schools.

held moral (religious) values of the students and their
parents. Since they espouse certain secular (anti-tradi-
tional) sexual values, it is also inevitable that they
should offend those who do not share their values. The
incompatibility between Roman Catholic teaching and
modern sex education is one example. During his visit
to the United States in 1979, Pope John Paul II reem-
phasized the moral illegitimacy of nonprocreative sex
and strongly condemned not only abortion but also
contraception. Not long after that papal visit, the Sacred Congregation for the Doctrine of the Faith, the
department of the Curia that deals with doctrinal devi-
ation, issued a sharp condemnation of a "liberal" Catholic sex manual, titled *Human Sexuality: New Direc-
tions in American Catholic Thought*. Although this
book was commissioned by the Catholic Theological
Society of America and was written by Roman Catholic
priests, it was found unacceptable by the Vatican because its authors "failed to accept the established
Catholic view that procreation is the central purpose of
human sexual activity."[15] Since contraception is one of
the central values in the sex education programs that
prevail in American schools today, the fundamental
incompatibility between such sex education and the
Catholic sexual ethic is clear.

The type of sex education acceptable to Catholics is
illustrated by the manual titled *Sex Education and
Training in Chastity*. Writing in 1930, the author, Father Felix M. Kirsch, emphasizes that sex hygiene
books written by non-Catholics "should not be recommended to our Catholic people."[16] Concerning what
should be taught the young about sex, Father Kirsch

writes: "In giving sex instruction to the young, we should never bring out the fact of the pleasure associated with sexual acts."[17] Although Father Kirsch views the control of the sexual impulse as a moral problem, he is quite willing to enlist the help of the physician to control it: "The priest should be familiar with the means recommended by the authorities on mental hygiene and physical health as these may assist the penitent in the fight against the sinful habit [masturbation]."[18]

Dispensing this sort of sex education today—in the United States or in the free West—would be unthinkable. (It would be possible to do so in Russia and China, provided the doctrine were identified as Communist rather than Catholic.) A public school teacher hectoring students about the wickedness of lust, masturbation, and fornication would be laughed out of the school system—if he was lucky. If he was unlucky, he might be locked up in a madhouse. With the sexual Jesuits thus routed, the schools are an easy prey for the sexual Jacobins, as the following stories illustrate.

In 1972, a group of high school students in Belfort, France, who were studying the writings of Sigmund Freud and Wilhelm Reich, asked their teacher to discuss a pamphlet entitled "Let Us Learn to Make Love," by a French physician, Dr. Jean Carpentier. The teacher agreed. The result was a huge public outcry, because Dr. Carpentier was "an outspoken advocate of unrestrained sexual self-expression. His pamphlet explains to high school students how their sexual organs work and urges free use of them in defiance of what he terms 'hypocritical moral authority' depriving

SEX EDUCATION—FOR CHILDREN   121

the young of pleasure."[19] How should students use
their sexual organs? The doctor recommends "love-making between boys and girls and also gives high marks
to homosexual relations and masturbation." There is, he
writes, "only one danger—the repression of desires."
Enraged parents accused the instructor of teaching
debauchery.[20]

The second story concerns an incident in West Berlin, reported in 1970. A group of schoolchildren in that
city, ranging in age from eight to fourteen, were "encouraged by scientists of the Free University to undress and enact scenes of sexual intercourse."[21] Why
did these German sex educators want children to do
this? Their purpose, they said, was "to emancipate
working-class children from the repressive influence of
their home education by exposing social exploitation
and sexual compulsion."[22] The teachers, described as
"members of a tightly knit extreme-leftist group that is
seeking to introduce international socialism," carried
out their experiments in a "Red Freedom storefront
center in a working-class district," without obtaining
the parents' permission for this exercise.[23]

These examples illustrate the many hidden moral
and political dimensions of sex education at the grade
and high school levels.

The situation with respect to sex education in the
schools may be clarified further by taking a quick look
at the leading American institution devoted to promoting such education—the Sex Information and Education Council of the United States. Founded in 1964
by Dr. Mary Calderone, a physician and former direc-

tor of the Planned Parenthood Association, the sustaining faith behind SIECUS is Calderone's missionary dedication to take sex away from the divines and give it to the doctors. At the celebration of the tenth anniversary of SIECUS, in a conversation with Harry Henderson, the editor-in-chief of *Medical Tribune*, Calderone made this quite explicit:

> HH: As I recall it, your original purpose was to link sex with health.
> Dr. C: Yes, and that turned out to be wise because it took sex out of the realm of morals. Fundamentally, sex has always been preempted by the religions and everybody kept hands off. By putting it into the area of health, where it scientifically belongs, by recognizing its role in physical, mental, and social well-being, we immediately freed it for objective, less emotional study and consideration.[24]

This is the characteristic rhetoric of scientism and statism: take whatever people do from whoever controls it, and give it to "science" and the state to control it on their behalf. Calderone's claim that "recognizing sex as an area of health" was an innovation for which she deserved personal credit and that looking at sex medically "frees it" and "makes it objective" is at once presumptuous and absurd. Physicians have been looking at sex medically for millennia. This has not resulted in clear-cut liberation from sexual repression; instead, it has resulted in countless people being sexually categorized, condemned, and controlled by means of pseudomedical ideas and interventions. Can anyone really believe that the lexicon of "sadism" and "masochism," of "vaginismus," "frigidity," and "impotence," of the countless "perversions," and of "castration anxiety" and "penis envy" has freed people?[25] The fact is that for more than a century psychiatrists have diagnosed people as sexual deviates, perverts, and psychopaths, and have assisted the law enforcement agencies of society in persecuting and punishing individuals so stigmatized.[26]

Phrases such as "sex is a health entity" and "sex is a key element of health" are typical of Calderone's cant.[27] What sex education should consist of, what young people should be taught and encouraged to do or not do—about all that, Calderone is confused and hypocritical. On one occasion she declares that she is "not suggesting the distribution of . . . contraceptive information to teenagers"[28]—that is, not even to adults of eighteen and nineteen. On another occasion she asserts that "sexual self-determination is clearly what sex education is all about" and enthusiastically endorses a 1974 World Health Organization resolution to the effect that "every person has the right to receive sexual information. . . ."[29] This inconsistency is characteristic of Calderone's sexological posturing.

Calderone's motivation for her crusade—to impose a therapeutically defined sexual "freedom" on people—is her business. However, when she foists her motivation on the public, it would be foolish to ignore it. What drives her, she says, is her desire to make the world a sexually better place for the generations to come. "What kind of sexual persons would we like our children, grandchildren, great-grandchildren to become?" she asks. Her answer is revealing: "We would hope that they are *not* to be: furtive, leering, guilt-ridden,

pathetic, compulsive, joyless. In other words, not like
ourselves!"[30] Is Calderone contemptuous of herself, of
her audience, or of both? If she herself is leering, guilt-
ridden, and (sexually) joyless, as she so arrogantly
confesses to be, then why should we accept her as an
expert on sexuality? And if she is not, then why should
we believe her?

One of the most remarkable and revealing facts
about Mary Calderone, the founding mother of modern
sex education, is the fact that she is against giving
teenagers—that is, even eighteen- and nineteen-year-
old persons—contraceptives or even contraceptive
information![31] Alas, she thus epitomizes the modern
medical sex educator who, under the guise of natural
science and liberal permissiveness, tries to prevent the
young from learning the truth. Mary Breasted, the author of a devastating exposé of SIECUS and sex education, concluded that "Mary Calderone et al. couldn't be
trusted to tell the truth about anything other than the
strictly biological material."[32] But teaching the strictly
biological material is the last thing Calderone wants to
do. What she really wants is to promote the religion of
the new psychiatric sexology. "In a few days [writes
Breasted] Mary Calderone would tell me that her goal
was 'sexual sanity' for America. And that was it; that
was what had put sex education into the schools."[33]

Insofar as the sex educators are successful in defining
themselves as the apostles of "sexual sanity," they also
succeed in defining their opponents as insane bigots.
"Sex education," declares Calderone, "is the best issue
the right wing has discovered in years, and they're
exploiting it for all it's worth."[34] With the leading edu-

cational and medical organizations squarely supporting sex education, it is not surprising that its opponents are dismissed as cranks and crazies.

This tactic points up one of the most objectionable aspects of sex education, ignored by most of its critics— namely, its intimate connection with psychiatry. The connection between psychiatry and sex education is deplorable, first, because it helps to foster the impression that anyone opposed to the sexual values advocated by the sex educators is opposed to mental health and science—from where it is but a small step to impugn the critic's sanity; second, because making sex education a matter of psychiatric concern strengthens psychiatry's weakening medical legitimacy and its shaky economic and social foundations. Among all the medical specialties, psychiatry is the only one whose job is to stigmatize people with moral judgments camouflaged as diagnoses and to imprison them under the guise of treatment. Entrusting matters of sex to this profession betokens our society's continued desire to stigmatize and suppress sexual interests and acts, and to do so under the cloak of medical management.

Still, we might ask: Why must sex education in the public schools be an intellectually and morally corrupt enterprise? Why could students not be taught, truthfully, how people multiply—just as they are taught, truthfully, how numbers are multiplied? There are two simple answers to these questions.

First, there can be no real sex education so long as it is called sex education. Arithmetic is not called banking education or gambling education and is not taught with an eye toward indoctrinating students into be-

coming bankers or gamblers. It would be possible to
teach students the facts (and prevailing hypotheses)
about the anatomy and physiology of the human sexual
organs, about contraception and abortion, and so forth.
But, as we have seen, sex educators do not want to im-
part *information*—they want to exert *influence*.

Secondly, sex education is doomed to be a corrupt
enterprise so long as it is taught within our present system of public education. Because the public school system is a tax-supported institution that possesses subtle
powers to coerce parents as well as children, it carries
in its bosom the danger of politicizing whatever it
touches. The risk of thus corrupting education in-
creases as we move from the hard natural sciences toward the soft social sciences. When it comes to sex education, the risk turns into reality. The fundamental
trouble with sex education in the public school system
is that it replaces biology and ethics with a particular
sexual ideology. That the sexual ideology it promotes
offends many people is an additional problem. Although Mary Breasted presents a devastating exposé of
sex education in the public school system, it does not
occur to her, as Ralph Raico points out, "that the very
existence of a controversy over sex education is due to
the fact that the government owns and operates the
schools." From that fact Raico cogently draws an infer-
ence whose importance extends far beyond the controversy over what teachers tell students about sex—
namely, that the government ownership of schools
makes "what would otherwise be an ordinary cultural
question (like whether women should wear miniskirts
or people should engage in group sex) into a political

question, where contending sides struggle for control of the state apparatus."[35]

Thus, it is precisely because sex education in the public schools is inexorably a political matter that its proponents find it necessary to deny its moral dimensions and to affirm its medical pretensions.

8

SEX EDUCATION—
FOR DOCTORS

Sex education is now an integral part of the curriculum of American medical schools. In January 1978, a state law became effective in California mandating education in human sexuality for all new physicians and surgeons seeking certification.[1] Immediately, the law generated heated controversy about what type of human sexuality training physicians need. This is hardly surprising: the activities now passed off under the rubric of sex education rival the idiocies that have been, and continue to be, promoted under the rubric of mental health or psychiatry. Nor is the connection between these two disciplines a coincidence: the two are often taught by the same people.

Of course, not everything taught as sex education to

medical students is offensive or useless. Some of it may
be reasonable enough. Typically a medical school offers
a single required course in human sexuality that covers
sexual biology, normal and abnormal sexual behavior,
psychosexual development, sexual disorders, and
treatment.[2] However, under the cover of such programs altogether different kinds of materials and
methods are introduced into the medical curriculum.
The materials include films and slides which, if shown
outside of medical schools, would be considered pornographic and possibly illegal. The methods include
procedures intended to "shock" and "reprogram" the
students and modifications of the target audience, extending the sexological instruction to nonstudents as
well. Because showing pornographic films is such an
important part of sex education in medical schools, the
subject deserves special consideration.

According to a 1975 article in *Medical World News*—
illustrated by the picture of a nude couple covered by
the legend "Joy in her pleasure," a dramatic symbol of
the crass sexism pervading medical sexology—"erotic
films play a significant part in the learning process at
most medical schools these days."[3] What is the ostensible purpose of showing such films to medical students?
To give experiential as well as informational knowledge, say the experts:

> Students are seated comfortably in a room with projec-
> tion screens all around them. They have been told that
> the session will be followed by a small group discus-
> sion. The lights go down, recorded music starts, and an
> incredible variety of sexual behavior is projected onto
> all the screens simultaneously—heterosexual inter-

course in many positions, fellatio, cunnilingus, homosexual intercourse, masturbation, sadomasochism.[4]

The idea of *showing* something to medical students
has obviously captivated the sex educators—offering
them a method that allows them to appear to be like
the other medical scientists and educators. The pathologist shows the student lesions, the microbiologist
shows him bacteria, the radiologist shows him X-ray
films—and the sexologist shows him pornographic films:
"Pornography appeared to be most useful as a part of a
multi-media blitz (sometimes called the Fuck-O-
Rama) which explored a broad range of sexual behavior through multiple projection of films with no emo-
tional or relationship elements."[5]

Sex educators claim that showing such films in medical school constitutes a special educational enterprise
called Sex Attitude Restructuring (abbreviated to
SAR).[6] The exercise is deemed therapeutic for the students, making them more objective toward their patients' sexual problems. Calling the use of pornographic
movies by a fancy name, like Sex Attitude Restructuring, is a feeble linguistic trick that requires no further comment. Claiming therapeutic benefits for such
movies is an exercise in hypocrisy, as reference to testimony given in a 1977 Florida trial concerning the ship-
ping of allegedly obscene films to Atlanta illustrates.

The object of the trial was a series of films titled
David's Boys, "five reels . . . showing young males enthusiastically engaged in the three most common
methods of homosexual lovemaking, plus a fourth,
more unusual technique."[7] The prosecutor contended

that the films were obscene. The defense countered that because the films were "therapeutic," they were not obscene. Testifying for the defense, Dr. Jay Mann, a psychologist-sexologist, offered this explanation of the value of the film to the jury: "In the same way aspirin eases a headache and penicillin battles the flu, a dose of pornography can work medicinal magic on sufferers of sexual stress. . . . These films can be used to promote sexual health."[8] Dr. Victor Cline, an expert witness for the prosecution, testified that the films were "medically sick as well as psychologically sick."[9] He claimed that the only people who engage in acts such as depicted in the films "are psychotics or people with brain damage."[10] Furthermore, said Cline, not only were the films "sick," they also caused "sickness": "Many rapists and child molesters say they imitated acts they have viewed on pornographic films. . . . Monkey see, monkey do. There is real danger in imitation."[11]

Defense and prosecution alike based their arguments not on moral but on medical grounds. If the films are "healthy" or "therapeutic," then they are not obscene and not illegal, they argued; and if they are "sick" or "pathogenic," then they are obscene and illegal.*

Actually, the use of pornographic movies for sex education in medical schools—institutions that might be ex-

---

* One of the jurors remained unpersuaded by these medical metaphors. (Perhaps he also knew that penicillin was ineffective against the flu.) Instead of finding the film therapeutic, he found it toxic: "One man disgustedly turned his head away from the courtroom movie screen until U.S. District Judge William Terrell Hodges told him to watch."[12]

pected to maintain a measure of academic dignity—is
objectionable on several grounds. I have already remarked on the moral grounds for such objection. The
practice is objectionable also on aesthetic grounds—
that is, because such films uglify sex and showing them
in medical schools uglifies medical education. Lastly,
the practice is objectionable on medical or scientific
grounds—that is, because pornographic films usually
present an inaccurate picture of the nature of sexual
acts between human beings.

The typical pornographic film shows one person sexually stimulating another person—"filling up" the stim-
ulated person with sexual arousal until he or she "produces" an ejaculation or orgasm. The participants may
also be shown to engage in such acts reciprocally. In
any case, the model is that of giving or getting an
enema—efficient erotic (genital) friction representing
water, the sexual organs and orifices representing the
rectum, and sexual release (ejaculation/orgasm) representing the successful delivery of a bowel movement.
One of the ways this imagery is conveyed is by showing a sexually experienced person (adult) giving a sexually inexperienced person (child) a "sexual enema."
Another way is by showing men and women giving
themselves "sexual enemas"—that is, using their partners as sources of sexual stimuli with which they fill
themselves until they are ready to have one or more orgasms. The result is the utter deprivatization of the
most intimate of all human acts—transforming sexual
acts between human beings into, and representing
them as, animalistic performances in which having a
good orgasm is like having a good bowel movement.

Still, the fact remains that many people are interested in, and enjoy, watching pornographic films. It
seems fairly obvious that they do so not because they
find the films educational but rather because they find
them sexually stimulating. However, as all human acts
(and even social contexts) have meaning, such films
must also teach something, and it is important that we
recognize what that is. First, they teach that "it's okay"
to have sex and to have it in the ways shown in the
film: the movie itself—but especially the fact *that* it is
shown and *where* it is shown—gives permission to the
audience to engage in the acts portrayed. Sex educators
often acknowledge that this is their primary aim in
showing such films. Second, pornographic movies teach
the viewer that the person doing the sexual stimulating in the film is a competent sexual performer—a
"teacher," or "therapist"; and that the person receiving
the sexual stimulation is a receptive sexual partner—a
"student," or "patient." (The metaphors of education
and therapy are here often interpreted literally, a
blurring essential to the purposes of sex education.)

In addition to relying on showing pornographic
films, the promoters of sex education for medical students have introduced another sexological teaching
method—namely, including the student's sexual partner
in the course. This practice is based, according to Herbert E. Vandervoort, director of the Human Sexuality
Program at the University of California in San Francisco, "on the assumption that the shared experience
will improve the couple's sexual interaction and thus increase the student's level of comfort with sexuality."[13]

This is typical of a sexological style that has hardened into medical-educational dogma. For example, the Program in Human Sexuality at the University of Minnesota Medical School is described as offering the same instruction and the same rationalization for it: "Each seminar brings together 80 persons, including the 'significant other' (spouse, fiancé, or friend) of the student or professional. Sprawled out on a large pillow, they watch films. . . . As many as six sexually explicit films [are] projected simultaneously on one wall of a university research building while pulsating rock music blares out."[14] The aim of this program, co-sponsored by the Minneapolis chapter of the American Lutheran Church, is "to desensitize participants about sex. . . ."[15]

Extending sex education to the medical student's sexual partner (or alleged sexual partner—for how could the instructor ascertain who these persons really are?) represents an invasion of the privacy of both of the people involved. The practice also rests on a questionable premise—namely, that the sex educator is sexually more competent than the students and their partners.†

One of the medical sex educators' favorite claims is that their methods—especially showing films depicting all manner of sexual acts—constitute "sexual desensi-

† A survey of physicians' life-styles, conducted by *Medical Economics* in 1979, revealed that psychiatrists had the most "unsatisfactory sexual relationships" (31 percent of the respondents). Psychiatrists also led the list of medical specialists having family problems due to "doctor's extramarital romance," "spouse's extramarital romance," and "doctor's drinking habits."[16]

tization and demythologization."[17] Perhaps such teaching does make medical students less sensitive to the importance of traditional sexual values. Whether that is a
desirable goal of medical education is, however, surely
debatable. In any case, calling such an enterprise demythologization is absurd. It is exactly the opposite.
Like mental health education or drug education, sex
education is a massive economically, ideologically, and
politically motivated myth-making. In fact, sex education rests on a systematic misrepresentation of moral
judgments about erotic practices as sexual diseases or
treatments. This misrepresentation begins with the dis-
tortion of language itself—for example, calling pornographic films used in sex education programs in medical
schools "graphic" or "sexually explicit media."[18]

In 1971, the prestigious Josiah Macy, Jr., Foundation
sponsored and subsequently published a *Macy Conference on Family Planning, Demography, and Human
Sexuality in Medical Education*.[19] This publication,
edited by the Dean Emeritus of the Yale Medical
School, may be taken as presenting and promoting the
best there is in American medical sex education. In the
report, John W. Money, professor of medical psychology at Johns Hopkins Medical School and one of the
leading American sexologists, writes:

> As an instructional device, a pair of movies, one show-
> ing clumsy and the other skilled erotic technique, can
> be beneficial adjuncts in the treatment of copulatory
> maladaptations between partners, including perfunc-
> tory and apathetic sex, faked orgasm, premature ejacu-
> lation, and impotence. At the present time, the primary
> source of such movies is the pornographic market. As

> a consequence they do not teach the precise lesson
> needed, matched exactly to each patient-couple's diag-
> nosis, as would be the case if sex films could be pro-
> duced by professionals for the commercial market
> through regular channels of distribution.[20]

The aim is for medical students, as well as patients,
to be taught how to perform the sex act *correctly:* "The
next step in the history of sexological medicine will
quite probably be the use of videotape to record errors
of relationship, including the errors of sexual performance, in a couple whose marriage is failing on a sexual
basis. With an actual record available the couple will
be able to compare their own inept approach to one another as compared with standards in demonstration
films."[21] Money is utterly serious, and quite humorless,
about all this—so much so that he makes not the
slightest allusion to the possibility that some individuals or couples might *want* their marriage to fail; that
they might *attribute* its failure to sexual incompatibility; and that there would be no way of discover-
ing this for anyone—unless the married couple revealed
the information. But it is really too much to expect that
Money should know this—because, as a psychologist,
he is even more hell-bent on medicalizing sex than the
psychiatrists he imitates.

It is both funny and frightening, but Money's final
recommendation is actually the establishment of a National Institute of Sex. Well, why not? We have National Institutes of Arthritis, Cancer, and Mental
Health. Since sex is a disease, or a treatment, or prefer-
ably both, it too deserves a National Institute. Such an
institute, says Money, "would function as an agent of

social change toward a more sane and healthy attitude toward sex and sexual behavior than our society at present enjoys."[22]

This leads us to the question of how we would identify or recognize a sane or healthy attitude toward sex? The experts—in particular John Money—would tell us. His ideas on this subject were expressed with admirable candor and great modesty in his testimony on behalf of Mature Enterprises, Inc., the defendant in an obscenity trial for showing the film *Deep Throat*. Testifying in Criminal Court in Manhattan in January 1973, Money declared, under oath, that viewing *Deep Throat* "could have a 'cleansing action' on people's sex lives."[23] The film, he maintained, had social value because seeing acts of fellatio and cunnilingus "would help remove inhibitions and mental blocks. . . . Couples would get so much joy in each other that they wouldn't keep discarding partners to seek pleasure in someone else."[24] Cross-examination did not shake Money's testimony. In reply to questions put to him by Assistant District Attorney William O. Purcell, Money asserted that less than one quarter of 1 percent of the people viewing *Deep Throat* would go back to see it "again and again." Money called these viewers "pictophiliacs," or picture freaks, "[who] were victims of a psychosexual disorder in which sexual satisfaction would come from viewing films."[25]

Unfortunately, we are not told how Money knows that the repeated viewing of *Deep Throat* is a symptom of mental illness, but the repeated performance of the acts depicted in it is a sign of mental health. Nor are we told how Money distinguishes "pictophiliacs" from "pictophobiacs." These omissions are especially regrettable in view of Money's sure grasp of how to identify the normal viewer of pornography. "Normal people," he asserted, "would become 'satiated' with explicit sexual films after two to four hours of exposure. . . . He estimated that 80 percent of men but few women 'in our duplicitous society' had reached such a stage of satiation."[26]

Not since the days of phlebotomy and phrenology has such drivel been taught in American medical schools—purveyed as medical science and paid for by the American taxpayer.

There is a profound ambivalence toward and confusion about "sexual freedom" and "sex crime" which pervades modern medical sex education—manifested by sex educators preaching sexual freedom while supporting "sexual psychopath" laws. The volume titled *Human Sexuality*,[27] published by the American Medical Association, displays dramatically this fatal inconsistency in medical sex education.

The value of "sexual psychopath" laws, say the authors, lies "in regarding the sexual psychopath as a mentally ill person instead of a criminal and in prescribing treatment rather than punishment. . . . Sexual deviates are clearly sick in the sense that they are caught up in behavior patterns they cannot control."[28] However, there is not a shred of evidence that "sexual deviates" are less able to resist their erotic preferences and rituals than devoutly religious persons are able to resist their theological preferences and rituals. It is, of course, precisely the act of categorizing certain persons

as sexual psychopaths that makes them appear in the
light in which this name is intended to show them—and
it is precisely this propensity to defame and dehuman-
ize persons who engage in "deviate" sex acts that the
sex educators show no sign of relinquishing.

Writing in 1972, the AMA's Committee on Human
Sexuality endorses a view about "perversions" and a
policy toward "perverts" that reveals the puritanism
and paternalism of its authors—and of the authorities
that continue to distribute, mandate, and approve medical sex education in the United States. Citing with
unqualified approval the views of the psychiatrist who
was one of those responsible for Ezra Pound's involun-
tary psychiatric hospitalization,[29] the authors of *Human Sexuality* declare that "Many of the persistent sexual offenders, notably those who engage in so-called
paraphilic ('perverted') practices such as homosexuality
. . . are mentally abnormal. . . ."[30] The authors call
for the indeterminate imprisonment (they call it "segre-
gation") and compulsory treatment of such persons—
adding that "treatment failing, [the sex offenders] may
be continued in confinement,"[31] presumably for life.

Some sex educators now proclaim that "There is no
norm in sex. Norm is the name of a guy who lives in
Brooklyn."[32] Others continue to claim that sexual de-
viations are mental diseases whose victims ought to be
confined and compulsorily treated.[33] Despite such glar-
ing inconsistencies, sex education is now a respected,
well-funded, expanding part of the medical curriculum.

No patriotic physician now questions the proposition
that doctors do not know enough about sex. Unrelent-

ingly, the experts assert that "physicians have inadequate medical school training in the management of
patients with sexual problems,"[34] that "doctors are
woefully ignorant about sex,"[35] and that "medical
workers are ill-equipped, educationally and culturally,
to give patients with sex-problems advice."‡ [36]

Ironically, the more sex is viewed as a medical matter, the more people expect doctors to be experts on
sex. Resting on false premises, this perspective could
only lead to more dissatisfaction by patients over their
physicians' incompetence to help them solve their sexual problem—and to an ever-increasing demand for
more sex education for physicians. This is why—despite
decades of intensive sex education, from grade school
through medical school—there is now a booming business in postgraduate sex education as well. It is a business, moreover, with which the general reader is not
likely to be familiar, since both its providers and con-
sumers are physicians and other health-related professionals.

The ostensible purpose of sex education courses for
physicians is to enrich their knowledge about human

---

‡ Even if it is true that medical students and physicians do not know
enough about sex, it does not follow that they should be taught more
about it. Doctors also do not know much about economics and law.
Should these subjects, too, be taught to medical students? The answer
is, of course, no—because, in a specialized society such as ours, persons
other than doctors are available to teach economics and law. Similarly,
persons other than doctors—for example, parents, peers, lovers, poets,
pornographers, prostitutes—are available to teach sex. Why should doctors compete with or displace them? Modern sex educators fail to address themselves to this question, and with good reason. The mere act
of articulating the supposed need for sex education for doctors—much
less questioning that need—undermines the tacit contemporary tend-
ency to turn human problems into medical ones.

sexuality and so enable them to treat their patients suffering from sexual disorders. Actually, most physicians take sex education courses because doing so is an easy way of earning the continuing education credits necessary for relicensure by state medical boards and for recertification by medical specialty boards. In 1975, *Medical World News* ran a feature article on "Courses for Doctors on Human Sexuality."[37] The article listed— in effect, advertised—several such courses, which the American Medical Association legitimizes by recognizing them for "continuing education" credit. The American government legitimizes them, and the American taxpayer helps to pay for them, by supporting many of the sponsoring institutions and by granting income tax deductions to the participants. Fourteen courses were listed for the period covering seven months, from March to October 1975. I will identify only a few of them, and those only partially—by title, date, and sponsor, omitting other information irrelevant to our present purpose.

POSTGRADUATE WORKSHOPS ON HUMAN SEXUAL FUNCTION AND DYSFUNCTION
June 9–14, August 18–23, October 20–25
Reproductive Biology Research Foundation, St. Louis

SEXUAL ENRICHMENT FOR PHYSICIANS AND SPOUSES
June 18
AMA Convention, Atlantic City

HUMAN SEXUALITY, July 26–27
Sponsored by the AMA's Regional Continuing Education Program, Minneapolis, Minnesota

SEXUAL PROBLEMS IN FAMILY PRACTICE
September 17–18
University of Michigan, Ann Arbor

In my files I have brochures of some of these courses and of many others. One was a "Sex Skill Workshop" sponsored by the American University and the American Association for Sex Educators and Counselors. Among the topics covered were "Current views on counseling homosexuals, transvestites, and transsexuals" and "Research on pornography and the law." Costs and credits were listed as follows: "273.00—three graduate credits and/or credit toward certification as AASEC certified sex therapist; $150.00—non-credit AASEC member; $160.00—non-credit, non-AASEC member."

Another was a course on "Sexual Dysfunction: Behavior Therapy Workshop," sponsored in Philadelphia by the Temple University Department of Psychiatry; in Boston by the Boston University Department of Psychiatry and the Princeton Center; and in Miami Beach by the Department of Family Medicine of the University of Miami School of Medicine and the Princeton Center. The cost ranged from $80 for one day, to $185 for two days and one evening, plus hotel expenses.

A more promising sex seminar was offered by Tropical Trips, a San Pedro, California, organization, in Puerto Vallarta, Mexico. Advertised as a "Professional Workshop on the Behavioral Treatment of Sexual Dysfunction, 8 days—7 nights," at a cost of $350 for double occupancy payable by Bank Americard, the course was good for twenty hours of Category 1 Credits in Continuing Medical Education, and twenty hours of Category A Credits toward the Certificate in Continuing Education in Psychology.

Another brochure advertised "A Professional Workshop on Sex Counseling Techniques for Health Professionals" sponsored by "The Travel Agents" of Los Angeles, California. This workshop—for "8 days—7 nights, from $670 double occupancy"—was scheduled aboard the *Song of Norway* cruising the Caribbean.

Such sex offerings are either held in the United States (and consist largely of indoctrination sessions into the methods of Masters and Johnson* or some other franchiser of sexual skills) or are held at resorts or aboard cruise ships (and are largely vacations laced with pornographic entertainment, sometimes enriched with opportunities for casual sexual game-playing). To award medical credits for this sort of thing brings discredit on the American Medical Association and the American medical community. To allow tax deductions for it makes suckers out of ordinary nonprofessional Americans.

There remains another category of postgraduate sex educational enterprises that deserves our critical attention: namely, the books, slides, and films—the so-called

---

* Masters and Johnson are among the principal beneficiaries of the continuing medical education industry, which is now a four-billion-dollar-a-year enterprise.[38] According to Leonard Fenninger, AMA vice-president for medical education, "Some CME programs are outrageously overpriced, while others do nothing to enhance the performance of physicians. There is no hard evidence that continuing education improves patient care, nor is it necessarily related to competence or ability."[39]

audiovisual materials—available to professionals only.

In 1974, the newspapers reported one of the highlights of the annual meeting of the American Psychiatric Association. A large photograph showed a group of men looking at an exhibit bearing the legend: "SEXUAL MATERIALS—VIEWING RESTRICTED TO APA MEMBERS ONLY." The caption explained:

> RX FOR SEX
> A color film exhibiting a couple making love draws in doctors shoulder to shoulder at the American Psychiatric Association's annual meeting in Detroit. The most popular exhibit at the gathering, the film is called "therapeutic audiovisual material for professionals" and has a clinical sound track explaining the scene. For sale only to professional groups, the films cost between $95 to $265. UPI Photo†[40]

A medical magazine, *Sexual Medicine Today*, has carried advertisements for such films defined as "sexual therapy aids." One firm offers "Sexual Therapy Film Programs . . . designed to help you counsel your patients easily and without embarrassment. As an adjunct

---

† Psychologists do not like to be outdone by psychiatrists. The 1974 annual meeting of the American Psychological Association thus offered similar entertainment for its members:

> "How-to-do-it" sex films were a central attraction in the exhibit area at this year's annual convention in New Orleans. At the EDCOA Productions booth shown above, standing-room-only crowds watched a small TV screen with clinical demure as a young couple demonstrated (in the words of an EDCOA brochure) "a series of sensate focus type exercises culminating in intromission in the female superior position." A slide show (on an even smaller screen) featured Relax and Enjoy It—an eight-minute film "depicting a young woman of average appearance masturbating to orgasm by means of digital manipulation."[41]

to sexual therapy, these explicit, color motion picture programs reinforce your personal counseling. . . ."[42] The distributor, called Professional Research Incorporated, offers a free projector and two free films to doctors who can place their orders by calling a toll-free telephone number.

The Multi Media Resource Center in San Francisco offers similar merchandise—fully described in connection with an article on the treatment of premature ejaculation. One film, titled *The Erogenists*, in color and sound, is advertised as follows: "A man demonstrates how to give a woman a full-body massage. Particular attention is focused on the female genital area. The film is useful to show couples how to teach each other and achieve intimacy without intercourse." Another film, titled *Give and Get*, is offered as a companion piece to *The Erogenists*. In this film "a woman massages a man, paying particular attention to his genital area. After she stimulates him to erection, the couple, in their mid 30s, move to a water bed for mutual caressing that concludes with intercourse."[43] If theater owners show such films to the public—that is obscenity; if sex therapists show them to patients—that is treatment.

Pornography—packaged in clinical terminology and labeled "for professionals only"—is a big business. The nature of the wares offered is illustrated by the advertisements for them. For example, one "Film Catalog"— distributed by the "Center for Marital and Sexual Studies," at Long Beach, California—offers films such as the *"Female Sexological Examination. . . .* The depiction shows a non-medical procedure with emphasis on

perception, feeling, and response of female genitalia. . . ." In sound and color, it rents for $65 and can
be bought for $395. The other films bear titles like
*Male Sexological Examination, Hand Caress, Face Ca-
ress,* and *Body Caress.* One is titled *Female Masturbation,* and is described thus: "This film depicts a female pleasuring and caressing various parts of her body
including her genitalia manually while looking at herself in a mirror. She then experiments with several vibrators and finally has a pronounced verbal outbreak as
she experiences orgasm." In sound and color, this film
rents for $60 and can be purchased for $275.

Another film, titled *Fun,* shows "a young couple engaged in intercourse on a waterbed. It depicts the fun
they have during foreplay and intercourse with some
laughing and play." This black-and-white film rents for
$75 and sells for $395.

Here is another—trivial but typical—example of what
passes for postgraduate sex education. The object
came through the mail, as do many of the things forbidden to laymen which doctors receive merely by virtue of their professional status. It is a brochure distributed by one of the oldest and most prestigious medical
publishers in the United States, the Williams & Wilkins
Company of Baltimore, Maryland.[44] It contains a "cen-
terfold" of four pages, on pastel blue paper (in contrast
to the white of the rest of the flier), offering a narrated
slide-tape or filmstrip of heterosexual intercourse (abbreviated as H.I.), which may be had for only $75. For
somewhat more, $180 to be exact, one can get the same
thing in color and sound film. If one is not interested in
intercourse, there is also a color sound film of mutual

masturbation. But it is not called that. It is called *Manual Stimulation,* abbreviated as "M.S.," and is described as follows: "Color sound film depicting the spontaneous acts of male and female in satisfying the partner. 11 minutes in length." There is an order form from which one may choose any item, or buy both "H.I. and M.S." in 16 mm color sound film for only $400. The last page of the centerfold completes the ritual of the medical ceremonializing of pornography. "The distribution of this program," we are informed, is limited to "professionals actively engaged in therapy, counseling, education, and/or research, . . . [and] accredited medical schools, graduate schools, universities, colleges, medical societies, hospital clinics, and schools of nursing."

This is crass discrimination. Architects and automobile manufacturers are excluded. But how can one perform H.I. or M.S. without a room or at least a car? Furniture designers and manufacturers are excluded. But, surely, H.I. and M.S. require a proper operative setting for the necessary organs and orifices.

Alas, all this sex education has not made doctors more competent to counsel their sexually troubled patients. Nor has it made them more knowledgeable about sex. A 1979 survey—sponsored by the American Academy of Family Physicians, with 900 physicians responding—revealed that 2 percent of the doctors believed that masturbation caused "physical harm"; 3 percent, that heterosexual intercourse did; 9 percent, that oral sex and extramarital sex did; and 23 percent, that homosexual practices caused such harm.[45]

Although the instructional value of postgraduate sex education is dubious at best, its impact on the personal morality of the doctor is likely to be deleterious. Both the content of the sex educational material directed toward the physician and the context in which it is delivered promote a loosening of traditional sexual morality—without offering alternative standards of personal conduct in its stead. The result is that the sexual abuse of female patients by male physicians, which has always been something of a problem in medicine, has, under the guise of "love therapy," probably become more common and surely more callously rationalized.

It is, of course, impossible to document that the frequency of this abuse has increased over what it was a decade or two ago. However, the frequency of newspaper and television stories about it suggests that that might very well be so. A steady stream of such stories has been reported by the press, in this country and Western Europe. From Germany comes a report about a Turin psychiatrist arrested with a suitcase full of nude photos of his female patients. The doctor defended himself against the charges lodged against him by claiming that the pictures served a "therapeutic purpose." After putting his female patients to sleep with drugs, he would act as "porno-photographer." Explained the doctor: "I showed the pictures to my patients to help free them from their inhibitions."[46]

A special session of the 1977 annual meeting of the American Medical Association was devoted to the subject of "sexual transgressions between physician and patient." Among the cases reported were that of a psy-

chiatrist who administered electric shock treatments
to a female patient and had sexual intercourse with her
while she was unconscious; that of a physician charged
with having sexual relations with a sixteen-year-old patient who he insisted was psychotic, but a lie detector
test showed that she was telling the truth; and that of
an unmarried physician who became a "one-man in-
semination service," fathering several illegitimate children with patients.[47]

The speakers commenting on these incidents insisted
that "sexual activity between physician and patient
should be looked upon as pathological."[48] That is still
another moral cop-out. Doctors who behave this way
have lost their morals, not their minds. It is especially
revealing that the physicians remarking on these sexual
abuses ignore the doctor's violation of his contract with
his patient for a certain service—which, of course, is not
a sexual service. Instead of acknowledging that such
physicians are acting immorally or illegally, the commentators use these incidents as still another opportunity to make morals a medical matter. They define the
transgressions themselves as medical (psychiatric)
problems: "Physicians who engage in such activity are
often more disturbed and depressed, even to the point
of suicide, than the disturbed patients with whom they
may have sexual affairs."[49] Such remarks incriminate
the medical profession doubly—first, individually, of
taking sexual advantage of patients who seek their
help, and second, collectively, of evading their moral
responsibility to judge those who engage in such acts as
responsible malefactors rather than as irresponsible
madmen.

Some of the discussants went even further, offering an interpretation that is becoming increasingly more fashionable—namely, that "there may be instances in which sexual advances to the patient by the therapist may be therapeutic. Among the therapeutic intentions [said this speaker], are the promotion of self-esteem in individuals with inadequate concepts of themselves, and to break down inhibition and repression of impulses."[50] These are shameful rationalizations, typical of the justifications for sexual exploitation advanced by health professionals.

The portrait of the medical sex-educator (among whom I include clinical psychologists) that emerges is not a pretty one. A national survey of licensed psychologists, conducted in 1977, utilizing anonymous written responses, revealed that "more than one in 20 male psychologists has had sexual intercourse with patients [and] more than one in ten admitted other 'erotic contact.'"[51] (Sex between female psychologists and male patients was rare.) The therapists who engaged in such behavior justified it by "saying that sexual intercourse helped their patients resolve problems of inferiority feelings and doubts about sexual identity. It also helped patients understand the mechanics of sexual intercourse."‡ [52]

‡ Like the hygienic rationalization of religious dietary practices, the therapeutic rationalization of such "professional" sexual practices flies in the face of some embarrassing facts. A recent survey of the membership of the American Psychological Association concerning sexual contacts between psychology instructors (in graduate school) and their students revealed that 17 percent of the women respondents reported that, as students, they had "sexual contact (genital stimulation or intercourse) with at least one of their psychology instructors." The more recently the psychologist received her Ph.D. degree, the

Psychiatrists do a little better—or worse, depending on one's point of view. According to a 1973 survey, 10 percent of male psychiatrists "admitted to erotic practices with their women patients, half involving intercourse."[54] These revelations, reported at the 1976 annual meeting of the American Psychiatric Association, produced the usual self-justification. "It is possible," said one psychiatrist, "that sex may one day come to be seen as beneficial to a patient."[55]

That day may be nearer than we think. In 1979, a survey conducted by Sheldon Kardener and Ivan Mensh, two psychologists at the University of California at Los Angeles, revealed that in a sample of 460 physicians, 13 percent "admitted to erotic contact" with female patients, and 19 percent said "they actually felt this was useful to patients."[56]

This is intellectual bankruptcy compounded by moral paralysis. The assertion that sexual contact between male physician and female patient may be therapeutic for the patient is self-serving and stupid. Using it to justify such sexual contacts is illogical and immoral. Claims and conclusions about doctors dispensing sex—by prescription, as it were—should, if anything, be the beginning of moral reasoning about the subject, not the end of it.

---

greater was the likelihood of her having engaged in sexual contact with her teacher, "25% of all recent female graduates (six years or less) report[ing] such a contact with an educator."[53]

9

SEX AND THE
STATE

Today's sex educators are mistaken—because they treat people as if they were animals, forgetting that the ultimate organ of human sexuality is not the genital but the mind. They are also mendacious—because they claim to be value-free scientists when, in fact, they are value-laden moralists. This pretense is the very antithesis of science, whose first commandment is telling the truth.

Since human sexual behavior is culturally shaped, anyone who writes about it must do so from a particular ethical and political perspective. My own belief is that spiritual and bodily self-ownership is a basic human right—perhaps the most precious of all human rights. From such a point of view, solitary sexual acts or private sexual acts between consenting adults are,

politically speaking, analogous to religious practices.*
Judging such acts legitimate or illegitimate, much less
prohibiting them by means of criminal (or mental
health) laws, falls outside the proper scope of government. The care and control of the sexual life of children is a responsibility of parents (and parent surrogates) and should also fall outside the scope of the
criminal law. Sexual relations between adults and children below a certain age should be illegal—the age
depending on the standards of the community.

There is no need, at this point, to belabor the influence of the Church on Western sexual beliefs and
practices during the better part of the past two thou-
sand years. The dominion of the theologians over sex
has now been largely replaced by the dominion of the
therapists. Of course, the clinicians maintain, just as did
the clergymen, that their aim is not to dominate or
coerce, but only to inform and help. Their behavior,
however, belies their claims. Neither theologian nor sex
educator is satisfied with conveying information; each
aspires to controlling conduct. As formerly the theological perspective on eroticism generated the dream of a
sexually virtuous society and justified the religious control of sex—so now the therapeutic perspective on eroticism generates the dream of a sexually healthy society
and justifies the medical control of sex.†

* This position in no way diminishes the right, indeed the responsibility, of individuals and of voluntary associations to form their own
ethical and aesthetic judgments about various types of human sexual
acts.
† For example, Masters and Johnson acknowledge that "One of
[their] most prominent concerns was the demand to develop a psychosocial rationale for *therapeutic control* of unmarried men and women
that might be referred for treatment" (emphasis added).[1]

The writings of modern sex educators and therapists are characterized by a grave inconsistency, amounting to deception: while seemingly supporting "sexual liberation," many of them actually advocate the most far-reaching methods of social control over human sexuality. For example, Robert Harper proposes, on the one hand, that "parents . . . encourage, help, and foster sexual play in their pre-adolescent children"—and, on the other hand, that "the only solution [to the population problem] is to take away the right to reproduce. . . . Placing long-lasting contraceptives in water supplies, staple foods, or oral time capsules is neither so radical nor so impractical as it first seems."[2]

Robert Chartham, a well-known British sexologist, preaches the same gospel of sexual freedom *and* the state control of sex. "Group sex," he declares, ". . . forces copulation from the close confines of man plus woman, husband plus wife, marriage plus family, into the free expression of our basic nature."[3] The "basic aim and the very foundations" of the sex education program that Chartham proposes is to remove "all fears and doubts about the propriety and validity of all the sexual manifestations of which the human body is capable." To achieve this repellent, but fortunately impossible, goal, Chartham suggests the following program: "If we eat together, swim together, discuss music, literature, sports and politics together, discuss sex together and have it demonstrated to us in the company of others, we cannot but accept it as a natural and normal human function."[4] Sex educators apparently do not understand or do not care what the political preconditions for, or consequences of, their policies might be:

in other words, that such a radical transformation of sex from a private into a public act would entail the end of individual freedom and dignity.

The idea that an exuberantly free sexual life might go hand in hand with an exceedingly unfree existence has, however, not escaped the imagination of great writers. Aldous Huxley describes precisely such a society in *Brave New World* (1932). The essence of Huxley's cautionary message is simple: modern science and technology might be harnessed to create a world populated by human beings that are happy slaves. But isn't that an oxymoron, an internally contradictory idea? How can one be unfree and happy? So it seems to the Savage (who speaks with Huxley's voice) too. His guide sets him straight. "Awful? *They* don't find it so. On the contrary. They like it. It's light, it's childishly simple. No strain on the mind or muscles. Seven and a half hours of mild, unexhausting labor, and then the *soma* ration and games and unrestricted copulation and the feelies. What more can they ask for?"[5]

In a foreword written to a new edition of this work in 1946, Huxley comments about the likelihood of his fears for the future coming true. His remarks seem even more cogent today than they were when they were offered—a third of a century ago:

> Nor does the sexual promiscuity of *Brave New World* seem so very distant. . . . *As political and economic freedom diminishes, sexual freedom tends compensatingly to increase.* . . . In conjunction with the freedom to daydream under the influence of dope and movies and the radio, it will help to reconcile [the

dictator's] subjects to the servitude which is their
fate. [Emphasis added.][6]

The world Ira Levin envisions in *This Perfect Day*
closely resembles Huxley's *Brave New World*. In his
medically managed "utopia" too, unrestricted copulation is a universal practice, serving as a sort of sexual
lobotomy.[7] What sensitive writers like Huxley and
Levin tell us—what such writers have always told us—is
that human beings are not animals or machines, and do
not want to be treated as if they were. A simple message, perhaps, but one that evidently needs to be constantly repeated—if for no other reason than to oppose
the Circean call of the sex educators whose charac-
teristically dehumanizing voices I shall, in conclusion,
recall once more.

In 1964 Alice Taylor Day, a prominent family planner, offered these prediction-prescriptions for population control in America: ". . . compulsory sterilization
following the bearing of two children would be one
such means; another would be to permit childbearing
to only a limited number of the adult population, all
the rest being sterilized."[8]

Alan Guttmacher, a famous obstetrician-gynecologist
who had been one of the most influential propagandists
for the "pill," was an outspoken advocate of state coercion for curbing overpopulation. "Each country," he
declared in 1969, "will have to decide its own form of
coercion, determining when and how it should be employed. The means presently available are compulsory

sterilization and compulsory abortion." He predicted that in the foreseeable future "a way of enforcing compulsory birth control will be feasible."‡ [9]

Language is, indeed, the fingerprint that those who write about human affairs leave behind. By means of that incorruptible self-identification, we can know them as they really are. Mary Calderone, the Circe of modern sex education, sings this—to many, apparently seductive—song: "If mankind as it now exists is obsolescent, then what kind do we want in his place and how do we design the production line? . . . In essence, that is the real question facing those concerned with sex education." [11]

Designing the production line for a new man and woman has, indeed, always been the favorite pastime of tyrants and their toadies. Hostility to that passion had inspired Voltaire, who said, "Theology is to religion what poisons are to food." [12] The same hostility has inspired this work and my conclusion that, paraphrasing Voltaire, sexology is to human sexuality what slavery is to freedom.

But freedom implies responsibility—in this case, each person's responsibility to confront his own sexual nature; to relate it to his vision of himself—in the present and the future; and to construct and conduct—from

‡ Alan Guttmacher's identical twin, Manfred Guttmacher, one of the leading forensic psychiatrists after the Second World War, was an ardent supporter of the coercive control of so-called sex offenders. "If it is considered the will of the majority," he wrote, "that large numbers of sex offenders . . . be indefinitely deprived of their liberty and supported at the expense of the state, I readily yield to that judgment." [10]

youth, through maturity, to old age—a sexual life that is genuinely his own.*

* The masculine pronoun in this sentence is, of course, only a concession to common linguistic usage. Obviously, women share the same task. Indeed, for obvious biological and cultural reasons, this is now an even harder task for them than it is for men.

SEX
BY PRESCRIPTION

Since everyone (except ascetics) regards both sex and
knowledge as good things, how could anyone be
against sex education or sex therapy? As a humorist
might say: easily.

I have presented a good deal of evidence in this book
to show that contemporary sex education is a fraudu-
lent and mischievous enterprise—principally because
sex educators systematically misrepresent cultural con-
ventions and moral prescriptions as health facts, and
falsify biological and medical facts to conform to social
expectations. That is an empirical or practical reason
for objecting to sex education. But there is another,
more abstract but perhaps more important, reason for
objecting to it. This objection rests partly on the nature

of human life, and partly on the nature of teaching and learning.

Our human destiny requires that, in order to become men and women, we master a vast number and complexity of skills. That is why we have large brains, require a long period to grow to maturity, and can never safely stop learning. Among the things we must learn is how to perform sexually and how to enjoy our own, and our partner's, sexual experiences. Some people conclude that because sex must be learned, it must also be taught. This does not follow. There are many things that we must learn that we can learn better—or can learn only—if we are allowed to learn it in our own time, at our own pace, in our own way. Among these things, sexuality stands very high.

"You can't live another person's life" is a popular saying whose truth is accepted as self-evident even by people not especially concerned with freedom. Why should this be so? Because the idea that every person is an individual, who has a life of his own to lead, is deeply embedded in the spirit of modernity. This is exemplified by the intense sense of individuality that people derive from choosing their occupation and hair style, the color of their car and the length of their fingernails, their hobbies and religion. Since one of the most personal things about human beings is their sexual preferences and practices, telling someone how to conduct himself sexually is (potentially, at least) inconsistent with letting him discover and develop his own style of sexual behavior.

Some people, unsure about how to engage in sex,

want sex experts to teach or treat them—just as some
people, unsure about what work they should engage in,
want experts on career choice to counsel them. Insofar as such experts supply the client with information
which the client lacks but needs to make an informed
choice, the encounter makes good sense. However, usually this is neither the aim nor the outcome of such consultations. They serve, instead, to shift the responsibility for making a difficult choice—often involving not
only vexing moral issues but also unknowable contin-
gencies about the future—from the client to the expert.
In short, this sort of "professional help" is likely to constitute a moral cop-out for the client and collusion in it
by the expert. Sex education and sex therapy provide
people with a rich reservoir of socially legitimized evasions about how they should conduct their sex lives—
which may be the main reason why they are popular.

Before commenting on our basic alternative to engaging in such evasions of our ethical obligations
(mainly to ourselves), a few remarks on education are
in order. The most casual scrutiny of the educational
process reveals that there are many important things in
life that, quite simply, cannot be taught—but can be
learned. Who taught Shakespeare to write poetry,
Beethoven to compose music, or Henry Ford to mass-
produce automobiles? To dismiss these examples as the
achievements of geniuses would be missing the point—
which is that such achievements are not unlike those of
ordinary persons, only vastly superior to them. The fact
that the discoveries or innovations of so-called geniuses
do not fall into an altogether different class from the
work of ordinary mortals is supported by the ease with

which such discoveries and innovations are assimilated
—and then often surpassed.

What the exceptional achievement of the great artist
or scientist and the everyday sexual behavior of ordinary men and women have in common is that each is
an intensely and intimately personal affair. This connection suggests an important lesson—namely, that if
we want to do something well and want to enjoy doing
it (two things that often go together), then what
counts is not what we are *taught*, but what we *learn*.
The relationship between teaching and learning—as we
know only too well from personal experience—is much
more loose than we like to pretend. Teaching a subject
or skill to someone does not mean that he or she will
learn it. In fact, being taught something (especially by
compulsion) can be a powerful incentive for not learning it. Conversely, many subjects and skills can be
learned without the person having to assume the role
of student or subject himself to a formal educational
process. Moreover, many things cannot be taught at all,
or can be taught only in a very general or rudimentary
fashion, the student having to acquire and master the
skill for himself. This is true, more or less, for a wide
range of human activities—from driving a car to playing chess, from speaking or writing well to keeping a
neat home. It is especially true for so-called sexual
skills.

Thus, the fact that human beings must learn how to
express themselves sexually and how to enjoy their own
(and their partner's) sexual experiences does not mean
that the best way to bring about sexual competence is
by sex education. On the contrary, all the evidence

points the other way—namely, that sex is something that people should have an opportunity to learn about and learn to engage in, but that it need not be, and indeed should not be, formally taught.

Accordingly, the view I have put forward in this book has implications that extend far beyond *opposing* government-sponsored and taxpayer-funded programs of sex education and sex therapy. It implies, equally, *supporting* an economic, legal, and political order that allows the individual a maximum amount of freedom to learn about and engage in sexual activities. Once again we must here fall back on the parallels between religion and sex: people should be able to inquire into, learn about, and practice or reject sex as freely and with the same impunities as they can inquire into, learn about, and practice or reject religion.[1] Thus, to the question "How should people go about obtaining help for their sexual problems?" my answer is: "The same sorts of ways they go about getting help for their religious problems." In a theological society, people are expected to seek clerical help. In a therapeutic society, they are expected to seek clinical help. In a free society, they could seek help from whomever they wished. This would leave individuals free to choose the source of their sexual enlightenment and "training": some people might prefer to get their sex education and sex therapy from "professionals," while others might choose books and pictures, parents and peers, friends and lovers, pornographers and prostitutes.

Hence, there can be no such thing as a single or even a few scientifically proven sex therapies for so-called

sexual dysfunctions. For the remedies will have to be
as varied as the individuals who display and diagnose
the problems. Many of my critics have asserted that I
deny the *reality* of various human problems (such as
family conflicts, the use of certain chemicals, or crime—
when I deny only that these phenomena are diseases).
But I do not deny that sexual problems exist or are real.
People have problems with their mothers and fathers,
their occupation or work, their leisure and recreation,
their children, their finances—so why shouldn't they
also have problems with their sexuality? I maintain only
that such problems—including sexual problems—are integral parts of people's lives. Indeed, whether a person
views a particular aspect of his own behavior *as a problem* itself depends on, and reflects, the sort of person
he is. In addition, whether he views the problem *as an
illness*, calling for medical attention—or as a personal,
moral, religious, or some other difficulty, calling for
quite different kinds of interventions—also depends on,
and further reflects, the sort of person he is.*

As some of the examples cited in the book illustrate,
one medical epoch's or person's sexual problem may be
another epoch's or person's sexual remedy. Today, it is
dogmatically asserted—by the medical profession and
the official opinion-makers of our society—that it is
healthy or normal for people to enjoy sex, that the lack
of such enjoyment is the symptom of a sexual disorder,

* Similar considerations apply also in cases of ordinary medical diseases, but the dissonance between professional and lay judgment is
often less conspicuous in that area than it is in areas where non-
organic conditions are defined and treated as if they were medical
illnesses.

that such disorders can be relieved by appropriate medical (sex-therapeutic) interventions, and that they ought, whenever possible, to be so treated. This view, though it pretends to be scientific, is, in fact, moral or religious: it is an expression of the medical ideology we have substituted for traditional religious creeds.

Sexual problems and the remedies for them, as I have tried to show, are as old as mankind. A brief concluding reference to, and remark on, one of the most famous cases of sex therapy in all history—dating back to the beginning of Christianity—may be instructive. The case is that of St. Augustine (354–430), one of the Fathers of the Roman Catholic Church. In his *Confessions*, Augustine gives a matchless account of his efforts to change his sexual orientation and practices from what they had been in his youth to what he wanted them to be in his maturity and old age.

Augustine, it seems, suffered from a "disease of desire": he had fallen into the habit of enjoying sex too much. As the years passed and his wish to embrace Christianity gathered strength, he beseeched God to release him from his "fetters of lust."[2] He also sought help from his religious counselors and from his own efforts to learn new sexual habits. For many years his exertions were unsuccessful—for reasons he explained in a justly famed passage: "I had prayed to you for chastity and said 'Give me chastity and continence, but not yet.' For I was afraid that you would answer my prayer at once and cure me too soon of the disease of lust, which I wanted satisfied, not quelled."[3]

St. Augustine's sexual metamorphosis is, in my opin-

ion, a paradigm of a successful—though protracted—
case of sex therapy: the patient's initial condition,
which he regarded as undesirable, was engaging in
pleasurable sexual intercourse (about which he felt
guilty); the condition he sought to achieve, and eventually did achieve, was an even more pleasurable abstinence from engaging in sexual intercourse (about
which he felt some regret). Today, most sexually troubled men and women undertake the return journey:
never having learned well enough how to enjoy sex,
they aspire to experience and exult in the lust Augustine rejected.

To the surprise of many, even of those who should
know better, most people have even more trouble
grasping the delights of sex than Augustine had in letting go of them. Alas, what a sad commentary this is on
our present concept of human nature: for doesn't the
study of economics, of politics, and especially of history and religion teach us that most people most of the
time find it easier to relinquish difficult aspirations than
to struggle to attain them? If this is true for being a
good son or daughter or parent, a good student or
teacher, a good friend, a good worker—then why
should it not be true also for being a good sexual partner? Few modern men or women believe that if they
engage in certain sexual acts they will go to hell when
they die, or that if they renounce sex altogether they
will go to heaven. But many seem to believe that if
they read the right sex manual, seek the counsel of the
right sex therapist, or find the right partner, then they
will enjoy unremitting sexual satisfaction, in a loving

encounter with another, with integrity and dignity, day after day, year after year, for forty, fifty, or more years. The absurdity of this image is a measure of the absurdity of modern sex education and sex therapy.

Notes

PREFACE

1. St. Augustine, *Confessions*, trans. R. S. Pine-Coffin (Harmondsworth, England: Penguin, 1978), p. 169.
2. H. S. Kaplan, Interview, *Medical Aspects of Human Sexuality*, November 1979, p. 26.
3. See, generally, H. S. Kaplan, *Disorders of Sexual Desire* (New York: Brunner/Mazel, 1979).
4. Quoted (in a slightly different translation) in R. E. L. Masters, ed., *Sexual Self-Stimulation* (Los Angeles: Sherbourne Press, 1967), p. 335.
5. See T. S. Szasz, *The Manufacture of Madness: A Comparative Study of the Inquisition and the Mental Health Movement* (New York: Harper & Row, 1970), Chapter 11; also this volume, Chapters 2 and 5.

Chapter 1
SEX AND THE SELF

1. See T. S. Szasz, "Pain in a New Perspective, 1975," in *Pain and Pleasure*, 2nd ed. (New York: Basic Books, 1975), pp. xi–xlvii; also, I. Singer, *The Goals of Human Sexuality* (New York: Norton, 1973).
2. C. A. Tripp, *The Homosexual Matrix* (New York: Signet, 1976), p. 118.
3. See T. S. Szasz, *The Myth of Mental Illness*, rev. ed. (New York: Harper & Row, 1974), especially pp. 1–13.
4. See I. Karacan, "Clinical Value of Nocturnal Erection in the Prognosis and Diagnosis of Impotence," *Medical Aspects of Hu-*

man Sexuality, April 30, 1970, pp. 27–34; C. Fischer et al., "Evaluation of Nocturnal Penile Tumescence in the Differential Diagnosis of Sexual Impotence," *Archives of General Psychiatry,* 36 (April 1979): 431–37.

5. See T. S. Szasz, *The Myth of Psychotherapy* (Garden City, N.Y.: Doubleday, 1978), Chapters 1 and 11.
6. Ibid., Chapters 2 and 3.

Chapter 2
SEX AS DISEASE

1. See O. Diethelm, *Medical Dissertations of Psychiatric Interest, Printed Before 1750* (Basel: Karger, 1971), pp. 61 and 66.
2. Ibid., p. 64.
3. See, generally, Szasz, *Manufacture of Madness;* and R. Hamowy, "Medicine and the Crimination of Sin: 'Self-Abuse' in 19th Century America," *Journal of Libertarian Studies,* 1 (Summer, 1977): 229–70.
4. B. Rush, *Medical Inquiries and Observations upon Diseases of the Mind* [1812]. Facsimile of the Philadelphia 1812 ed. (New York: Hafner Publishing Co., 1962), pp. 33 and 374.
5. Quoted in E. H. Hare, "Masturbatory Insanity: The History of an Idea," *Journal of Mental Science,* 108 (January 1962): p. 4.
6. Ibid.
7. Ibid.
8. Quoted in J. Duffy, "Masturbation and Clitoridectomy," *Journal of the American Medical Association,* 186 (October 19, 1963): 246.
9. R. V. Pierce, *The People's Common Sense Medical Adviser: In Plain English; or Medicine Simplified,* 71st ed. (Buffalo: World's Dispensary Printing Office and Bindery, 1895), p. 772.
10. Ibid., p. 785.
11. R. Krafft-Ebing, *Psychopathia Sexualis, With Special Reference to the Antipathic Sexual Instinct: A Medico-Forensic Study,* trans. F. J. Rebman from the 12th German ed. (New York: Paperback Library, 1965), p. 48.
12. Ibid.
13. Ibid., pp. 286–87.
14. Ibid., p. vii.
15. S. Freud, "Sexuality in the Aetiology of the Neuroses" (1898), in *The Standard Edition of the Complete Psychological Works of Sigmund Freud,* 24 vols. (London: Hogarth Press, 1953–74), vol. III, pp. 276, 278 (hereafter cited as SE).
16. See H. Nunberg and E. Federn, eds., *Minutes of the Vienna Psychoanalytic Society, Vol. II: 1908–1910,* trans. M. Nunberg (New York: International Universities Press, 1967); and H. Nunberg

and E. Federn, eds., *Minutes of the Vienna Psychoanalytic Society,
Vol. III: 1910–1911*, trans. M. Nunberg (New York: International
Universities Press, 1974).

17. S. Freud, "Contributions to a Discussion on Masturbation" (1912),
SE, vol. XII, pp. 250–52.

18. S. Freud, "The Unconscious" (1915), SE, vol. XIV, p. 200.

19. S. Freud, "Introductory Lectures on Psychoanalysis (1916–1917),"
SE, vol. XVI, pp. 309 and 316.

20. K. Menninger, *Man Against Himself* (New York: Harcourt, Brace,
1938), pp. 68–69.

21. C. W. Socarides, *Beyond Sexual Freedom* (New York: Quadrangle
Books, 1975), p. 88.

22. Ibid., p. 83.

23. Ibid., p. 89.

24. E. Halpert, "On a Particular Form of Masturbation in Women:
Masturbation with Water," *Journal of the American Psychoanalytic
Association*, 21 (1973): 526.

25. Ibid., p. 542.

26. P. Roth, *Portnoy's Complaint* (New York: Random House, 1969).

27. S. Hite, *The Hite Report: A Nationwide Study on Female Sexuality*
(New York: Macmillan, 1976).

28. W. Hunt, Review of *The Hite Report*, *Journal of the American
Psychoanalytic Association*, 26 (1978): 237–38.

Chapter 3
SEX AS TREATMENT—IN THEORY

1. Quoted in Diethelm, *Medical Dissertations of Psychiatric Interest*,
p. 91.

2. C. Riel, *Rhapsodien über die Anwendung der psychischen Cur-
methode auf Geisteszerrüttungen* [Rhapsodies About the Applica-
tion of Psychological Cures in Mental Disorders] (Halle, Germany:
Cutschen Buchhandlung, 1803), pp. 185–86. The translation is
mine.

3. *Time*, April 29, 1969, p. 51.

4. W. H. Masters and V. E. Johnson, *Human Sexual Response*
(Boston: Little, Brown, 1966).

5. *Time*, April 29, 1969, p. 51.

6. E. M. Brecher, *The Sex Researchers* (Boston: Little, Brown, 1969),
p. 287.

7. W. H. Masters and V. E. Johnson, *Human Sexual Inadequacy*
(Boston: Little, Brown, 1970), p. 3.

8. W. H. Masters and V. E. Johnson, "Principles of the New Sex
Therapy," *American Journal of Psychiatry*, 133 (May 1976):
548–54.

9. See F. A. Hayek, *The Counter-Revolution of Science: Studies on the Abuse of Reason* (New York: The Free Press, 1955), p. 154.
10. Masters and Johnson, *Human Sexual Inadequacy*, p. vii.
11. Ibid., p. 150.
12. P. Robinson, *The Modernization of Sex* (New York: Harper & Row, 1976), p. 123.
13. Ibid., p. 125.
14. G. Orwell, "Politics and the English Language" (1946), in *The Orwell Reader: Fiction, Essays, and Reportage* (New York: Harcourt Brace, 1956), pp. 355–66.
15. M. H. Hall, "A Conversation with Masters and Johnson," *Medical Aspects of Human Sexuality*, December 1969, p. 43.
16. See T. S. Szasz, *Karl Kraus and the Soul-Doctors: A Pioneer Critic and His Criticism of Psychiatry and Psychoanalysis* (Baton Rouge, La.: Louisiana State University Press, 1976), especially Chapter 3.
17. R. M. Weaver, *The Ethics of Rhetoric* (Chicago: Regnery, 1953), pp. 11–12.
18. Masters and Johnson, *Human Sexual Inadequacy*, p. 4.
19. Ibid., pp. 20–21.
20. Ibid., p. 21.
21. Ibid., p. 146.
22. Ibid.
23. Ibid., pp. 146–47.
24. Masters and Johnson, *Human Sexual Response*, book jacket.
25. W. H. Masters and V. E. Johnson, *Homosexuality in Perspective* (Boston: Little, Brown, 1979).
26. *Time*, April 23, 1979, p. 78.
27. Ibid.
28. Ibid.
29. Masters and Johnson, *Homosexuality in Perspective*, p. 227.
30. H. Marano, "New Light on Homosexuality," *Medical World News*, April 30, 1979, p. 13.
31. See B. Russell, "The Superior Virtue of the Oppressed," in *Unpopular Essays* (New York: Simon and Schuster, 1959), pp. 58–64; and T. S. Szasz, *Schizophrenia: The Sacred Symbol of Psychiatry* (New York: Basic Books, 1976), pp. 212–14.
32. Quoted in N. Gittelson, *Dominus: A Woman Looks at Men's Lives* (New York: Farrar, Straus & Giroux, 1978), pp. 50–51.
33. Masters and Johnson, *Human Sexual Response*, p. 213.
34. Ibid., p. 65.
35. Masters and Johnson, *Homosexuality in Perspective*, pp. 10–11.
36. Ibid., p. 31.
37. Ibid., pp. 27–28.
38. Ibid., pp. 54–55.
39. Ibid., p. 51.

40. Ibid., p. 403.
41. Ibid.
42. Ibid., p. ix.
43. Robinson, *The Modernization of Sex*, p. 162.
44. San Francisco Sunday *Examiner and Chronicle*, October 1, 1978, p. A-6.
45. Ibid.
46. Quoted in A. Butterfield, Jr., "Dr. Masters at Anaheim," *Psychiatric News*, June 18, 1975, p. 1.
47. Ibid., pp. 1 and 16.
48. Ibid., p. 16.
49. Ibid.
50. Ibid.
51. Ibid.
52. New York *Times*, January 14, 1975, p. 26.
53. M. Seligson, "Orgasms for Sale," *Reflections*, 10 (1975): 4–5.
54. *Time*, June 14, 1974, p. 90.

Chapter 4
SEX AS TREATMENT—IN PRACTICE

1. Quoted in the New York *Times*, June 23, 1975, p. 28.
2. Ibid.
3. Quoted in *Medical Aspects of Human Sexuality*, 7 (August 1973): 159.
4. *Süddeutsche Zeitung* (München), August 1, 1978; *Abendzeitung* (München), August 8, 1978. The translation is mine.
5. Masters and Johnson, *Human Sexual Inadequacy*, p. 369.
6. Ibid.
7. L. Wolfe, "The Question of Surrogates in Sex Therapy," in J. Lo-Piccolo and L. LoPiccolo, eds., *Handbook of Sex Therapy* (New York: Plenum Press, 1978), p. 492.
8. J. LoPiccolo, "The Professionalization of Sex Therapy," in ibid., p. 518.
9. Wolfe, "Question of Surrogates," p. 493.
10. Ibid., pp. 491–92.
11. Ibid., p. 495.
12. Ibid.
13. *Newsweek*, November 27, 1972, p. 71.
14. Wolfe, "Question of Surrogates," p. 495.
15. *Time*, September 10, 1973, p. 48.
16. Ibid.
17. *The Guardian* (London), July 10, 1979, p. 12.
18. Ibid.
19. *Newsweek*, November 27, 1972, p. 72.

20. "Valerie X. Scott" and Herbert d'H. Lee, *Surrogate Wife* (New York: Dell, 1971), back cover.
21. Ibid., p. 1.
22. Ibid., p. 20.
23. Ibid., p. 21.
24. Ibid., p. 8.
25. Ibid., p. 23.
26. Ibid.
27. Ibid.
28. Ibid., p. 32.
29. Ibid., p. 34.
30. D. H. Leroy, "The Potential Criminal Liability of Human Sex Clinics and Their Patients," *St. Louis University Law Journal,* 16 (1972): 589.
31. Ibid., p. 590.
32. Ibid., p. 592.
33. Ibid., p. 593.
34. Ibid., p. 595.
35. Ibid., p. 594.
36. Ibid., p. 595.
37. Ibid., p. 596.
38. I. Veith, *Hysteria: The History of a Disease* (Chicago: The University of Chicago Press, 1965), p. 38.
39. "Some Remarks on the Science of Onanism," in Mark Twain, *The Mammoth Cod, an Address to the Stomach Club,* with an Introduction by G. Legman (Waukesha, Wis.: Maledicta Press, 1976), p. 23. I wish to thank Mr. Frederick Anderson, literary editor of the Mark Twain papers, the University of California at Berkeley, and Professor Robert H. Hirt, Department of English, the University of California at Los Angeles, for calling my attention to this piece.
40. Masters and Johnson, *Human Sexual Inadequacy,* p. 369; see also Chapter 2 of this volume.
41. Masters and Johnson, *Human Sexual Response,* p. 125.
42. Masters and Johnson, *Human Sexual Inadequacy,* p. 240.
43. W. C. Lobitz and J. LoPiccolo, "New Methods in the Behavioral Treatment of Sexual Dysfunctions," *Journal of Behavior Therapy and Experimental Psychiatry,* 3 (1972): 267.
44. Ibid., p. 268.
45. J. S. Annon, *Behavioral Treatment of Sexual Problems* (New York: Harper & Row, 1976), pp. 113–14.
46. N. Lauersen and S. Whitney, *It's Your Body: A Woman's Guide to Gynecology* (New York: Grosset & Dunlap, 1977), p. 11.
47. Ibid., pp. 484–85.
48. "Questions and Answers: The Vibrator as a Therapeutic Sexual

Technique," *Journal of the American Medical Association*, 239 (May 1978): 2173.

49. "Seven Weeks to Sexual Health: The Loyola Sexual Dysfunction Clinic," *Sexual Medicine Today*, October 1979, pp. 9 and 28–29.

50. See, for example, L. G. Barbach, *For Yourself: The Fulfillment of Female Sexuality* (New York: Signet, 1975), p. 87.

51. M. Weisberg and B. Whitney, "Sexual Medicine: Masturbation," *The New Physician*, March 1978, p. 36.

52. M. S. Calderone, quoted in W. H. Masters et al., eds., *Ethical Issues in Sex Therapy and Research* (Boston: Little, Brown, 1977), p. 47.

53. H. H. Sewell, "Sexual 'Norms' in Marriage," *Medical Aspects of Human Sexuality*, 8 (October 1974): 84.

Chapter 5
SEXUAL SURGERY

1. See B. Bettelheim, *Symbolic Wounds: Puberty Rights and the Envious Male* (Glencoe, Ill.: The Free Press, 1954).

2. Genesis 17:9–14.

3. I Samuel 18:25–27.

4. D. Gross, ed., *Dictionary of the Jewish Religion* (New York: Bantam, 1979), p. 54.

5. *Code of Jewish Law: A Compilation of Jewish Laws and Customs by Rabbi Solomon Ganzfried*, trans. Hyman E. Goldin, rev. ed. (New York: Hebrew Publishing Co., 1961), vol. 4, p. 44.

6. R. L. Baker, "Newborn Male Circumcision," *Sexual Medicine Today*, November 1979, p. 35.

7. A. Cohen, *Everyman's Talmud* (New York: Schocken, 1975), p. 381.

8. Ibid., p. 382.

9. F. C. Forberg, "Masturbation in Classical Erotology" (1884), in Masters, *Sexual Self-Stimulation*, p. 333.

10. I Corinthians 7:17–18.

11. Matthew 19:12.

12. See T. S. Szasz, *Heresies* (Garden City, N.Y.: Doubleday Anchor, 1976).

13. See Chapter 2; also Szasz, *Manufacture of Madness*, Chapter 11, and Hamowy, "Medicine and Crimination."

14. Quoted in A. Comfort, *The Anxiety Makers: Some Curious Preoccupations of the Medical Profession* (London: Nelson, 1967), p. 108.

15. Quoted in Masters, *Sexual Self-Stimulation*, pp. 43–44.

16. J. Crosby, quoted in Masters, *Sexual Self-Stimulation*, pp. 41–42.

17. G. J. Barker-Benfield, *The Horrors of the Half-Known Life: Male Attitudes Toward Women and Sexuality in Nineteenth-Century America* (New York: Harper & Row, 1976), p. 125.
18. R. A. Spitz, "Authority and Masturbation: Some Remarks on a Bibliographical Investigation," *Yearbook of Psychoanalysis* (New York: International Universities Press, 1953), vol. 9, p. 123.
19. Quoted in Barker-Benfield, *Horrors of the Half-Known Life*, p. 125.
20. F. R. Sturgis, "Treatment of Masturbation" (1900), in Masters, *Sexual Self-Stimulation*, pp. 36–37.
21. See Chapter 2.
22. L. D. Longo, "The Rise and Fall of Battey's Operation: A Fashion in Surgery," *Bulletin of the History of Medicine*, 53 (Summer, 1979): 244–67.
23. Ibid., p. 244.
24. Ibid., p. 249.
25. Ibid.
26. Ibid., p. 250.
27. Ibid.
28. Ibid., p. 256.
29. Ibid., p. 263.
30. K. Menninger, *The Vital Balance: The Life Process in Mental Health and Illness* (New York: Viking, 1963), p. 198.
31. C. W. Socarides, "Homosexuality," in S. Arieti, ed., *American Handbook of Psychiatry*, 2nd ed. (New York: Basic Books, 1974), vol. III, p. 301; see also C. W. Socarides, *Beyond Sexual Freedom* (New York: Quadrangle Books, 1975), especially pp. 96–112.
32. A. Waugh, "Sex in Britain," *Spectator* (London), December 8, 1979, p. 8.
33. J. Bremer, *Asexualization: A Follow-Up Study of 244 Cases* (New York: Macmillan, 1959), pp. 179–80.
34. Ibid., pp. 16–17.
35. See New York *Times*, December 23, 1973, p. E-9; and "Homosexuality," *Medical World News*, January 4, 1974, p. 4.
36. M. Annexton, "Treatment of Impotence by Penile Implants," *Journal of the American Medical Association*, 241 (January 1979): 13 and 17.
37. P. Albertson, "Treating Impotence with Surgery," *Sexual Medicine Today*, 2 (June 1978): 22.
38. Ibid.
39. *Time*, December 10, 1979, p. 92.
40. Ibid.
41. Ibid.
42. "The New Arterial Bypass That Reverses Organic Impotence," *Sexual Medicine Today*, January 1979, pp. 8–13.
43. *Time*, December 10, 1979, p. 92.

44. See J. G. Raymond, *The Transsexual Empire: The Making of the She-Male* (Boston: Beacon Press, 1979).

45. See *Hospital Tribune*, March 21, 1977, p. 3; San Francisco *Chronicle*, April 21, 1978, p. 2; and New York *Times*, May 16, 1979, p. A-19.

46. See T. S. Szasz, "Male Women, Female Men," *The New Republic*, October 9, 1976, pp. 8–9.

47. U. G. Turner, in "Transsexualism," *The Pharos*, 41 (October 1978): 33–34.

48. See Raymond, *Transsexual Empire*, and T. S. Szasz, "Male and Female Created He Them," New York *Times Book Review*, June 10, 1979, pp. 11 and 39.

49. S. Herschkowitz and R. Dickes, "Suicide Attempts in Female-to-Male Transsexual," *American Journal of Psychiatry*, 135 (March 1978): 368–69.

50. T. S. Szasz, "Equation of Opposites," New York *Times Book Review*, February 6, 1966, p. 6.

51. *American Medical News*, September 7, 1979, p. 18.

52. *Time*, August 27, 1979, p. 64; see also *Medical World News*, September 17, 1979, pp. 17–19.

53. D. Forester, quoted in *Medical Tribune*, October 24, 1979, p. 13.

54. H. Benjamin, quoted in *Sexual Medicine Today*, November 1979, p. 19.

55. *Medical World News*, April 17, 1978, p. 62.

56. D. E. H. Russell and N. Van de Ven, *Crimes Against Women: Proceedings of the International Tribunal* (Milbrae, Calif.: Les Femmes, 1976), pp. 151–52.

57. See T. S. Szasz, *The Theology of Medicine: The Political-Philosophical Foundations of Medical Ethics* (Baton Rouge, La.: Louisiana State University Press, 1977; New York: Harper Colophon, 1977).

Chapter 6
RELIGION AS SEX EDUCATION

1. D. M. Feldman, *Birth Control in Jewish Law: Marital Relations, Contraception, and Abortion as Set Forth in the Classic Texts of Jewish Law* (New York: New York University Press, 1968), p. 30.

2. Ibid., p. 37.

3. Quoted in ibid., p. 50.

4. Genesis 19:1–30.

5. Genesis 19:31–38.

6. D. Gross, ed., *Dictionary of the Jewish Religion* (New York: Bantam, 1979), p. 176.

7. L. M. Epstein, *Sex Laws and Customs in Judaism* (New York: Ktav Publishing House, 1967), p. 141.
8. Deuteronomy 7:3–4.
9. Cohen, *Everyman's Talmud*, p. 382.
10. Ibid., pp. 381–82.
11. Quoted in Feldman, *Birth Control in Jewish Law*, pp. 81–82.
12. Ibid., p. 89.
13. Ibid., p. 63.
14. Ibid., p. 64.
15. Syracuse *Post-Standard*, December 20, 1979, p. A-3.
16. Feldman, *Birth Control in Jewish Law*, p. 74.
17. Epstein, *Sex Laws*, p. 137.
18. G. R. Taylor, *Sex in History* (New York: Vanguard Press, 1970), p. 60.
19. Epstein, *Sex Laws*, pp. 133–34.
20. Feldman, *Birth Control in Jewish Law*, p. 114.
21. See, generally, ibid., pp. 110–65.
22. Epstein, *Sex Laws*, p. 147.
23. Ibid.
24. A. Edwardes, "Self-Stimulation Among Arabs and Jews," in Masters, *Sexual Self-Stimulation*, p. 308.
25. R. Briffault, *Sin and Sex* (1931), with an Introduction by Bertrand Russell (New York: Haskell House, 1973), pp. 69–70.
26. T. Besterman, *Men Against Women: A Study of Sexual Relations* (London: Methuen, 1934).
27. See, for example, D. S. Bailey, *Sexual Relations in Christian Thought* (New York: Harper & Bros., 1959), pp. 23–24.
28. Ibid.
29. Ibid., p. 46.
30. G. May, *Social Control of Sex Expression* (London: George Allen & Unwin, 1930), p. 38.
31. Bailey, *Sexual Relations*, p. 84.
32. Ibid., p. 171.
33. Ibid., p. 198.
34. Ibid., p. 235.
35. *Newsweek*, March 5, 1979, p. 101.
36. May, *Social Control*, p. 27.
37. Ibid., p. 24.
38. In this connection, see Szasz, *Heresies*.
39. May, *Social Control*, p. 39.
40. See T. S. Szasz, *Ceremonial Chemistry: The Ritual Persecution of Drugs, Addicts, and Pushers* (Garden City, N.Y.: Doubleday Anchor, 1976).
41. See, generally, A. Edwardes, *The Jewel and the Lotus: A Historical Survey of the Sexual Culture of the East* (New York: Lancer Books, 1965).

42. *The Koran*, trans. N. J. Dawood (Baltimore: Penguin, 1970), pp. 20–21.
43. Ibid., pp. 211–12.
44. Ibid., p. 212.
45. Cohen, *Everyman's Talmud*, p. 385.

Chapter 7

SEX EDUCATION—FOR CHILDREN

1. See *Newsweek*, June 2, 1969, pp. 66–67; and J. Kasun, "Turning Children into Sex Experts," *The Public Interest*, Spring, 1979, pp. 3–14.
2. Quoted in P. C. Beach and J. Likoudis, "Sex Education: The New Manicheanism," Parts I and II, *Child & Family*, 10 (1971): 242–59 and 314–29.
3. *Newsweek*, June 2, 1969, p. 66.
4. Citizens for Parental Rights (Schenectady, N.Y.), "These Are *Our* Children! They Do Not Belong to the State!" (Mimeographed, n.d.) See also Schenectady *Union-Star*, February 27, 1969, p. 2.
5. Citizens for Parental Rights, op. cit.
6. Quoted in Beach and Likoudis, "Sex Education," pp. 242–43.
7. Quoted in Kasun, "Turning Children into Sex Experts," pp. 3–4. I have relied on Jacqueline Kasun's review of sex education programs for several of my following examples.
8. Ibid., p. 4.
9. Ibid., p. 5.
10. Ibid., p. 11.
11. B. C. Gruenberg and J. L. Kaukonen, *High Schools and Sex Education*, Educational Publication No. 7 (Washington, D.C.: U. S. Public Health Service, 1939), p. 67.
12. *Medical World News*, July 23, 1979, p. 55.
13. Quoted in ibid.
14. New York *Times*, January 24, 1978, p. 18.
15. Quoted in the New York *Times*, December 9, 1979, p. 21.
16. F. M. Kirsch, *Sex Education and Training in Chastity* (New York: Benziger Brothers, 1930), p. 204.
17. Ibid.
18. Ibid., p. 280.
19. New York *Times*, December 26, 1972, p. 31.
20. Ibid.
21. New York *Times*, April 13, 1970, p. 12.
22. Ibid.
23. Ibid.
24. *Medical Tribune*, March 19, 1975, p. 14.

25. In this connection, see J. Hillman, *The Myth of Analysis* (Evanston: Northwestern University Press, 1972), especially pp. 140–42.
26. See Szasz, *Manufacture of Madness,* especially Chapters 10–14.
27. M. Calderone, "The Challenge of Our Sexual Future," *Sexual Medicine Today,* December 1978, p. 34.
28. Quoted in M. Breasted, *Oh! Sex Education!* (New York: Signet, 1971), p. 249.
29. Calderone, "Sexual Future," p. 34.
30. Ibid.
31. See Breasted, *Oh! Sex Education!,* p. 249.
32. Ibid., p. 357.
33. Ibid., pp. 311–12.
34. Quoted in the New York *Times,* May 20, 1969, p. 72.
35. R. Raico, Review of *Oh! Sex Education!, The Alternative,* January 1973, p. 16.

Chapter 8
SEX EDUCATION—FOR DOCTORS

1. M. Reik, "California Laws Mandate Sexual Education for All New Doctors," *Sexual Medicine Today,* February 1978, p. 14.
2. *Medical World News,* March 24, 1975, pp. 113–28.
3. Ibid., p. 113.
4. Ibid., pp. 121–22.
5. M. Briggs, "The Use of Audio-Visual Materials in Sexuality Programs," in N. Rosenzweig and F. P. Pearsall, eds., *Sex Education for Health Professionals: A Curriculum Guide* (New York: Grune & Stratton, 1978), p. 133.
6. Ibid., p. 131.
7. St. Petersburg *Times,* August 17, 1977, p. 4B.
8. Ibid.
9. Tampa *Tribune,* August 18, 1977, p. 2.
10. Ibid.
11. Ibid.
12. St. Petersburg *Times,* August 17, 1977, p. 4B.
13. *Medical World News,* March 24, 1975, p. 120.
14. New York *Times,* July 8, 1974, p. 21.
15. Ibid.
16. M. Kirchner, "What Makes Other Marriages Lousy," *Medical Economics,* October 1, 1979, p. 43.
17. See, generally, *Medical World News,* March 24, 1975, pp. 113–28, and Rosenzweig and Pearsall, *Sex Education for Health Professionals.*
18. H. E. Vandervoort and T. McIlvenna, "Sexually Explicit Media in Medical School Curricula," in R. Green, ed., *Human Sexuality: A*

Health Practitioner's Text (Baltimore: Williams & Wilkins, 1975), p. 235.

19. V. W. Lippard, ed., *Macy Conference on Family Planning, Demography, and Human Sexuality in Medical Education* (New York: Josiah Macy, Jr., Foundation, 1971).

20. J. Money, "Pornography and Medical Education," in ibid., p. 106.

21. Ibid.

22. Ibid., p. 108.

23. Quoted in the New York *Times*, January 3, 1973, p. 50.

24. Ibid.

25. Ibid.

26. Ibid.

27. *Human Sexuality* (Chicago: American Medical Association, 1972).

28. Ibid., p. 206.

29. See T. S. Szasz, *Law, Liberty, and Psychiatry* (New York: Macmillan, 1963), pp. 59–60, 67–69, 201–3.

30. *Human Sexuality*, p. 206.

31. Ibid.

32. A. Comfort, quoted in *Medical World News*, November 8, 1974, p. 115.

33. *Human Sexuality*, p. 206.

34. D. W. Burnap and J. S. Golden, "Sexual Problems in Medical Practice," *Journal of Medical Education*, 42 (July 1967): 673.

35. Ibid.

36. World Health Organization, quoted in *International Herald Tribune*, February 25, 1975, p. 8.

37. *Medical World News*, March 24, 1975, pp. 113–28; see also "Continuing Education Courses for Physicians, for the Period from September 1, 1978, Through August 31, 1979," *Journal of the American Medical Association,* 240 (1978): 901–5, 1037–66.

38. See J. J. Fisher, "Let's Stop Blowing Our Money on C.M.E. Ripoffs," *Medical Economics*, August 7, 1978, pp. 71–74; L. W. Ghormley, "I Call It Coercive Medical Education," ibid., pp. 74–75.

39. Quoted in *Medical Economics*, May 28, 1979, p. 13.

40. Sacramento *Bee*, May 9, 1974, p. A-4.

41. *APA Monitor*, 5 (November 1974): 3.

42. "Advertisement, for Physicians: Audiovisual Resources," *Sexual Medicine Today*, October 1978, p. 19.

43. Ibid.

44. *Psychiatry/Psychology* (Baltimore: Williams & Wilkins Company, n.d.).

45. *American Medical News*, July 6, 1979, p. 15.

46. *Süddeutsche Zeitung* (München), March 30, 1974. The translation is mine.

47. Boston *Herald American*, June 22, 1977, p. 2; see also *Medical World News*, September 3, 1979, pp. 38–39.
48. Boston *Herald American*, June 22, 1977, p. 2.
49. Ibid.
50. Boston *Herald American*, June 22, 1977, p. 2.
51. St. Petersburg *Evening Independent*, November 11, 1977, p. 5; for the full report, see J. C. Holroyd and A. M. Brodsky, "Psychologists' Attitudes and Practices Regarding Erotic and Nonerotic Physical Contact with Patients," *American Psychologist*, 32 (October 1977): 843–49.
52. St. Petersburg *Evening Independent*, November 11, 1977, p. 5.
53. *Roche Report: Frontiers of Psychiatry*, November 1, 1979, p. 3.
54. Los Angeles *Times*, June 5, 1976, p. 2; for the full report, see S. Kardener, M. Fuller, and I. Mensh, "A Survey of Physicians' Attitudes and Practices Regarding Erotic and Nonerotic Practices with Patients," *American Journal of Psychiatry*, 130 (October 1973): 1077–81.
55. Los Angeles *Times*, June 5, 1976, p. 2.
56. *Medical Tribune*, July 4, 1979, p. 17.

Chapter 9
SEX AND THE STATE

1. Masters and Johnson, *Human Sexual Inadequacy*, p. 146.
2. Quoted in Detroit *Free Press*, September 4, 1969, pp. 1-A and 9-A.
3. R. Chartham, *Your Sexual Future* (New York: Pinnacle Books, 1972), p. 73.
4. Ibid., pp. 120–21 and 183.
5. A. Huxley, *Brave New World* (1932) (New York: Bantam Books, 1955), p. 152.
6. Ibid., p. xiii.
7. I. Levin, *This Perfect Day* (Greenwich, Conn.: Fawcett/Crest, 1970), especially pp. 36–38.
8. A. T. Day, "Parenthood: Its New Responsibilities," *Smith Alumni Journal*, November 1964, quoted in Beach and Likoudis, "Sex Education," p. 252.
9. Quoted in the New York *Times*, July 6, 1969, p. 47.
10. M. D. Guttmacher, *Sex Offenses* (New York: Norton, 1951), p. 132.
11. Quoted in Beach and Likoudis, "Sex Education," p. 323.
12. Quoted in J. Orieux, *Voltaire*, trans. Barbara Bray and Helen R. Lane (New York: Doubleday, 1979), p. 349.

Chapter 10
SEX BY PRESCRIPTION

1. See, in general, T. S. Szasz, *The Theology of Medicine: The Political-Philosophical Foundations of Medical Ethics* (Baton Rouge, La.: Louisiana State University Press, 1977; New York: Harper Colophon, 1977).
2. St. Augustine, *Confessions,* p. 169.
3. Ibid.

Index

tence and prostheses for, 82–86; masturbatory insanity and, 75–80; modern, 75–96; oophorectomy, 78–80; the state (political philosophy) and, 94–96; transsexuals and, 86–92, 95

Surrogates. *See* Prostitutes

Surrogate Wife (Scott and Lee), 55–58

Talmud, 100, 102, 103, 105

Teachers (educators), sex education and sexology and, 115–27, 128–51, 152–58, 159–67 (*see also* Sex education; Sexology; Sex therapy; specific aspects); and relation between learning and teaching of sexual skills, 162; and scientism and statism, 115–16, 122–27, 152–58

Teenage sex education, 115–27. *See also* Sex education

Therapeutae, 109

Third World countries, clitoridectomy in, 93–94

This Perfect Day (Levin), 156

Time magazine, 28–29, 38, 47, 86 n

Torah, the, 103, 105

Transsexualism, 74 n, 86–92; sex-change surgery and, 86–92, 95

Transvestites, 81; sexual surgery and, 81–82

Tripp, C. A., 5 n

Tropical Trips, sex seminars offered by, 142–43

Twain, Mark, on masturbation, 62, 176

"Unconscious, The" (Freud), 21–22

Vagina, 29–30 (*see also* Genitals); reconstruction surgery, 93; transsexual surgery, 87–96

Vaginismus, 8, 12, 122. *See also* Frigidity

Vandervoort, Herbert E., 133–34

Vatican, and sex education, 119–21. *See also* Roman Catholics

Venereal disease, xv, 4 n

Vibrators, use of, 11, 64–65, 66–67

Vienna Psychoanalytic Society, 21

Virginity, religion as sex education and, 108, 111, 113

Voltaire, 157

Washington University, 58–59

Weaver, Richard, 33 n

Weisberg, Martin, 68

Whitney, Bobbie, 68

Whitney, Steven, 66

Williams & Wilkins Company (Baltimore, Md.), 146–47

Wolfe, Linda, 52–54

Women (*see also* Female sexuality; specific aspects, developments, groups, theories); and masturbatory orgasmic inadequacy, 63–64, 77 (*see also* Masturbation; Orgasm); and religion as sex education, 99–114 *passim;* and sex education and sexology (*see* Sex education; Sexology); as surrogates in sex therapy, 28, 31, 41, 47–48, 49–51, 52–61; and sex with counselors and psychology instructors, 148–51

World Health Organization, 123

Yahveh, 102, 104, 106, 112

Zohar, the, 105

Zorgniotti, Adrian, 86